WHITE HUNTER

WHITE HUNTER

The Adventures and Experiences of a Professional Big-Game Hunter in Africa

J. A. HUNTER

Safari Press Inc.
P. O. Box 3095, Long Beach, CA 90803

The trademark Safari Press ® is registered with the U.S. Patent and Trademark Office and in other countries.

Hunter, J.A.

Safari Press, Inc.

1986, Long Beach, California

ISBN 1-57157-122-1

10 9 8 7 6 5 4 3 2

Readers wishing to receive the Safari Press catalog, featuring many fine books on big-game hunting, wingshooting, and sporting firearms, should write to Safari Press Inc., P.O. Box 3095, Long Beach, CA 90803, USA. Tel: (714) 894-9080 or visit our Web site at www.safaripress.com.

DEDICATION

To the sportsmen and sportswomen
from all parts of the world with whom I have had the pleasure
of coming into contact during the last quarter of a century—I
dedicate this volume.

PREFACE

IVORY—twenty-four shillings per pound—such was Africa's lure! Who would not fall? Many hunters and others who had never shot an elephant were fascinated with the idea of trying their luck, bought a rifle and ammunition and set off to hunt. Licences were a nominal figure, and allowed for a big margin of profit on each elephant shot. It was when you reckoned— at least, I did—pound for pound, that bang went 1s. 6d., the price of a 450 No. 2 cartridge, the return on this being on an average £150, the price of two tusks.

Buffalo hides were also much in demand by the natives for making shields, and these commanded anything from £6 to £8 each. Then rhino horns were also a saleable commodity.

The results were that, from the hides and the rhino horns alone the elephant licences and expenses were paid. Quite a lucrative and thrilling type of employment.

I have written here of some of those trips when we had to take the good with the bad, the rough with the smooth. It was a hard life, but kept you fit, and there was always the expectancy of shooting something really big. Licences were limited, but there was always a way to get round this by purchasing permits for someone else and paying them a nominal fee for the privilege of using them.

Then, again, permits to export may have been used twice. Ivory has left ports in all disguises, even as cases of machinery, and also cut in lengths and soldered up in tins of ghee. The days of which I write are all of the past, when the grip of the law was not so stiff or binding; and now that the price of ivory has fallen so considerably, buffalo hides unsaleable, and the cost of licences on a higher scale, this all tends to prolong the life of the game which will continue to thrive, and Africa will rank as the world's greatest natural Game Park for generations to come.

I would like to tender my grateful thanks to the following: The Game Warden of Kenya, Capt. A. T. A. Ritchie, for allowing me to take figures and notes from his annual reports, especially on the poaching fraternity; the Earl of Winchilsea; Prince Adolph Schwarzenberg; Mr. Lea Hudson; and Allen McMartin of Montreal, for the use of photographs reproduced in this volume.

J. A. HUNTER.

NAIROBI.

LIST OF CONTENTS

LIST OF ILLUSTRATIONS
(FOUND BETWEEN PAGES 128-129)

YOUNG ELEPHANT BULL REFUSING TO LEAVE HIS COMRADE.
PHOTO BY PERSMISSION OF ALLEN A. MCMARTIN, MONTREAL.

RIVER SCENE, NORTHERN RHODESIA.
PHOTO BY PERMISSION OF ALLAN A. MCMARTIN, MONTREAL.

A FINE BLACK-MANED LION.
PHOTO BY J. A. HUNTER.

THE AUTHOR.
PHOTO BY LEA HUDSON.

CLOSE RANGE.
PHOTO BY PERMISSION OF ALLEN A. MCMARTIN, MONTREAL.

LUNCH IN THE SHADE.

LIONESS SCANNING THE VELDT.
PHOTO BY J. A. HUNTER.

A LIONESS POSING IN THE FORK OF A TREE.
PHOTO BY J. A. HUNTER.

THE BUFFALO SPOTTED US.
PHOTO BY PERMISSION OF THE EARL OF WINCHILSEA.

PUKU, NEAR LAKE RUKWA, TANGANYIKA.
PHOTO BY PERMISSION OF ALLEN A. MCMARTIN, MONTREAL.

15

List of Illustrations

WHITE HUNTER

C H A P T E R   *O N E*

Elephant

IVORY was still rising in value. A fellow hunter and myself discussed going after elephants while the going was good and decided to travel as light as possible, piling our blankets, rifles and food in a Ford box-body car. The distance ahead of us was roughly two hundred and thirty miles from the capital. At this time the roads were more or less mere tracks, and in the first hundred miles misfortune dogged us; it was discovered that my roll of blankets had fallen from the car. Doubling back to look for them, we found it to be a waste of time and petrol, as we passed several natives who declared they had not seen the missing bag; but natives love blankets, and I suppose you could not expect them to disclose their hidden treasure. Continuing our journey, we called at an Indian duka, where I purchased some blankets of inferior quality at enhanced prices, and we made our camp half-way to our favoured ground.

With an improvised rod and some line we strolled down to a stream and caught several fish, although poor fare, as they were of a cat- or mudfish variety and barbel. Here we shot an impala ram for food, as the flesh of this antelope is considered amongst the best in Africa.

Next morning we were early astir and breakfasted off our fish caught the previous evening and set off. The going was appalling—over partly made roads—the rain had washed deep ruts on either side and you dared not take your eyes from the route while driving. One stretch of twenty-seven miles took us four hours to accomplish—but then our thoughts ran to those elephants ahead, and when in this frame of mind all roads are good ! This track had been used by Indian merchants, who were trading with the inland natives, taking out sugar and other trade goods and returning with loads of cattle hides and sheep skins. It is surprising in so many of our East African territories to see these Indian traders setting up stores and trading there year in and year out. Even today there are many natives who have not yet seen any small town and are content to live and die in their own surroundings.

We arrived at our camp just as the sun was setting, and here we were, camped in a wooded valley, with quite a number of game in the vicinity. Several natives came along to our camp with the usual request—tobacco. These folks look on this as part and parcel of their daily life, just as much as many Europeans. They grow their own tobacco, dry it, and when completed it smokes vile—and smells worse. Enquiries about elephants elicited the information that there were many within a mile of where we stood.

Next morning, while eating a scanty breakfast, some blue monkeys chattered in a stream within a hundred yards of our tent. They kept looking down and were quite excited. My friend and self strolled towards them, and near the pool where our only porter had drawn water was a leopard spoor in the mud. Now the leopard was obviously hungry to be out looking for food at 8 a.m., and I suggested to my friend that he should proceed towards the foothill, where there were many oribi (small antelope), while I would fix up a gun trap, using my rifle to be fixed with a cord to pull the trigger. I heard two shots in the distance, and very soon an oribi was forthcoming. Taking out the kidneys and liver for ourselves, the carcase was placed inside the barricade, leaving an opening for him or her to enter. The rifle was adjusted to be fired on pressure by its head, being previously tested with the hand for correct tension. Within half an hour the rifle banged off, although the sound was muffled to a certain degree, as the rifle was fired towards the earth. Proceeding to the trap, we found one female leopard, dead, below the trap, shot through the back of the neck. I imagined I saw something else move in the bush as we came forward, and remarked to my friend, " What was that ?" Placing another cartridge in the breech, we had barely covered the hundred yards to our camp when another report was heard. Now, I thought, has some inquisitive native gone and inspected it and most likely placed his foot below it ? That is the danger with this type of trap.

Cautiously going forward, there was the male leopard dead, hunched up; he had died in exactly the same manner. This is the quickest time I have ever seen two leopards trapped, the time between each being twenty minutes.

That afternoon we strolled down to a large wooded ravine where, natives had informed us, elephants had been seen that morning. At 5 p.m. we were sitting on a little knoll, surveying the area, when the unmistakable sounds of branches being broken were heard, and made us realise that elephants were there. You could hear them in the centre of the bush, and from the branches moving it was evident they were feeding towards the edge, where we sat. While watching and hoping for a decent bull to show himself, two young bulls pushed their heads out and their white ivory shone in the setting sun. Eventually they came out in the open, followed by five more. The last one had thick, stained ivory, and my friend, not even rising, fired at him, hitting him behind the shoulder. They all crashed back into the bush whence they had emerged, and after a few minutes we decided to follow. Arriving at the place where the bush was brushed aside, we could not hear a sound, and my friend entered the bush all intent on looking for blood spoor. This was found only five yards inside. I, being close behind, glanced upwards, and immediately my eye caught the outline of the wounded bull standing, practically towering, over him. Grabbing my friend's coat, I pulled him back without courtesy, and even then he wondered why I had done so. Taking a second to explain, we went further along the bush, some twenty-five yards, and cautiously went in. From here we could see him; he had not moved and was supporting himself on the stem of a tree. Two quick shots and he sank, in fact slid, down that trunk. His tusks were just on the 80-lb. mark, and this was certainly easy hunting.

Returning to our camp well satisfied, the leopard trap was again visited, but we had evidently finished the family.

Next day we scouted round a large area of that valley. There were elephants everywhere, but, always waiting to see something better, we lost a good opportunity by waiting too long, as a fine bull stood facing us, showing good ivory, only it is easier to judge weights of ivory from a side view than from a frontal one. He disappeared into the thick bush and did not venture out on our side of the ravine. This day proved a blank.

Next morning we resolved to go in two different directions; I would try the lower end of the valley, while my friend would hunt the top. Coming to the edge of the ravine, I could see where they had caught the scent of our walking about the previous night, and I heard in the distance the short scream of a bull elephant quite a mile further down, and on the other side of the forest.

Hurrying down with a Masai, who was carrying my double rifle, we crossed over, and what a sight met our gaze ! All the elephants were commencing to trek up the side of the hill or escarpment, and were heading as though to leave the valley. It was a long, steep slope, and some of the animals appeared to be practically on top of the ridge. A great stand it would have been for anyone posted at the top of that worn-out trail. I used my binoculars and saw two good bulls behind, following up the main body, and I was determined to try and catch up with them. I had a Rigby ·350 magnum in my hand, and hurried on.

When I arrived at the foothill, my tusker was at least 200 yards ahead. Scrambling up that mountain-side was quite an effort and I was soon puffed, although my Masai did not seem to mind gradients. Even the elephant, I saw, had his rests, and when he was resting I was going, and *vice versa*. Midway up I knew it would be quite impossible to shoot accurately on account of the climb, but at length I actually came to within sixty yards of him. Whether he heard me or not, I do not know, but I have a recollection of seeing that bull turn and come down that hill—half sliding—but tearing on, boulders and stones creating a terrible din. There was a black jagged rock, four feet high, in front of me, and I rushed for that and fired as quickly as I could as he tore past on the path I had followed up. I hit him in the chest—I did not know just where, as my arms were very unsteady. He never faltered at the shot, but came past me, within a few yards. I tried to dodge further to the left and I saw his eyes as he passed, but in his mad rush he could not stop. Giving him another shot, I called for my other rifle —not a sign of my Masai, and then I saw an object half a mile away on the ridge—it was he and my

rifle ! This elephant continued for some distance
and then crashed, breaking one of his tusks against
the rocks as he fell. To see this huge form and hear
the noise of him coming down the hill were terrifying and I was lucky that the great herd ahead had
not stampeded; it numbered about 300. My friend
had a wonderful view of the whole hunt and afterwards informed me that the speed of the native and
the elephant, although going in different directions,
was similar.

On the following day we moved our camp in the
direction the herd had gone, pitching our tent near
a small stream. From here we had a wonderful
view of the surrounding country, mostly undulating
grassland, with isolated hills, which we could climb
and with binoculars scan the whole area for many
miles. Masai were grazing cattle on this plateau,
and evidently these natives did not view the
elephants living in their grazing lands with alarm.
Informing several herd boys that a reward of Rs. 5
would be given for information regarding any big
bulls, we soon had news.

About 2 p.m. a Moran, or young Masai warrior,
came along to say that he had seen a large elephant
in some high grass only one mile from our camp.
Hurrying to the place indicated, from a small
hillock the back of this tusker was quite visible.
He was big, but on account of the tall, coarse grass,
it was difficult to obtain a good view of the ivory he
carried.

My friend, when climbing the escarpment on the
way to the camp, had slipped on a rolling stone and

sprained his ankle, which made it quite impossible for him to accompany me. Proceeding in the direction of this elephant was more difficult than I had anticipated. Down in the valley I could see practically nothing, and the fine dust coming from the long grass made it anything but pleasant to walk through, and apart from that, the noise made in walking was against me. Turning back from this elephant grass, I resolved to try another move, and skirting round, I found a well-beaten elephant trail.

Following this, accompanied by my cook, who carried my ·577 rifle, I carrying a ·318 magazine, we soon heard the elephants in front of us, maybe seventy yards away. Reaching a small clearing where the grass had been trampled down by a small herd a few days previously, I could discern my prize. Rain commenced to fall and I saw him throw up his head, and his tusks were held high up above the grass. They were good as regards size and yellow in colour. Now I must get close to him, so I ventured further, but was beaten by the height of the grass, as it was obvious that unless I could reach within a few yards, I was not going to be able even to see this eleven-foot high monster. My cook boy following indicated the sound of some movement in the grass to our left, and here was a dilemma ! Should we be caught in a sort of trap ? We retraced our steps to the small opening behind us and not too soon. Within thirty yards there were several elephant cows coming straight to where we stood. Your brain works quickly in such a place—at least mine did—and I took hold of my

·577 and fired at the shoulder of the bull standing in the tall grass. You will invariably shoot high in grass, and I had the satisfaction of hearing the thud of my bullet on the elephant. Immediately I fired, the herd of cows crashed this way and that, and watching them, I entirely lost sight of the bull I had fired at. It was literally pouring now, and I was drenched to the skin, and wet khaki is about the most uncomfortable form of clothing I know.

Proceeding to where I had fired at the bull, there were the heavy impressions made by his feet when he tore off. Following the trail, blood was picked up on the sides of the tall grass. From the colour and froth, it was obvious I had hit him too high, the bullet getting the lung. Now I have found when elephants are hit through both lungs and have difficulty in breathing, they will not take to the higher ground. This bull had gone at great speed and actually did top one ridge, proving that only one lung was hit.

Determined to get him, we followed on, and for the first mile he did not even slow down. Passing under the slope of a hill, where several old trails converged, I had the misfortune to go headlong into a disused game pit. At the bottom of this I sat down to recover myself, the drop had been so sudden. My old cook boy with some difficulty extricated me; but for his help I would have had much trouble, owing to the sides tapering down to a wedge shape. When I finally did get on top again, I felt it was quite impossible for me to follow on, and I wondered how I would ever make the camp some three miles behind me. My old cook volunteered to carry on and follow for an hour or so, while I trudged back to camp, a forlorn and crestfallen hunter! I reached there with difficulty, and here were the two of us, both on the maimed list.

While I was recounting my experiences that afternoon, some Masai brought further news of elephants to the south of us, and we had unfortunately just to grin and bear it. That night there was no sign of my old cook. The Kisii tribe at this time were inclined to be truculent, and I wondered if he had run foul of them, as the elephant was heading in their direction. The next morning I felt better, and my Masai rubbed my shoulder and side with fat of some description. The " massage " administered made me squirm, but I felt better for it, even though their methods are drastic.

Mentioning their doctoring reminds me of the time when one of my porters had an offending back tooth and my old Masai was requisitioned as the dental surgeon. I was interested in this method of extraction, and will explain the procedure as I witnessed it. Making the boy lie down on his back, he opened his mouth and produced a hard piece of wood, scooped out to hold the side of the tooth. Pressing this against the tooth, he used a stone as a mallet, and sure enough out went that tooth at the first blow. It was the most drastic of any form of surgery I have seen, and he afterwards slated the boy for being such a coward as to flinch, but then these Africans generally seem immune to pain, compared with the European. It is the same with medicine ; the hotter, the more vile tasting or stringent in their way of thinking is the only one which will effect a cure. Concentrated vinegar, I found, appealed to the Masai most ; this, to their mind, banished all diseases and complaints.

Returning to my narrative. Twenty-four hours had elapsed since my cook had vanished, and I made up my mind to leave next morning at day-break, as I now felt fit enough, and see if I could not trace him. If the elephant was dead, the vultures soaring above the carcase would give us direction and a clue as to its whereabouts. About 6 p.m. that same evening, however, there was my faithful old cook heading back to the camp from the op-posite direction, and with the aid of binoculars I could see he was carrying something in his hand. As he came nearer, it was real good to see that it was the tail of my elephant.

His story was interesting. He came up with the elephant standing in an open valley, quite unable to go further, and he emptied the magazine in its direction at a long distance, but he was afraid none of the bullets hit, as he was too far away. He was now with an empty rifle and it was a relief to him when the elephant crashed down and died. Afraid of the Kisii natives with their long-shaped spears, and of the animals, he had trekked through the night, getting quite lost, and had gone to sleep in the early hours of the morning, not waking up until nearly two that afternoon, when he saw in the distance the small curl of smoke coming from our camp fire.

Leaving next morning, we came up with the carcase and found some natives removing the last of
the elephant's bones.   With the promise of more
meat they were persuaded to assist in carrying the
tusks, which scaled in at 85 and 83 lb. each, to the
camp.

Reports then began to come in daily from different natives, all bent on securing the Rs. 5 premium.
Amongst the most promising reports was that from
two warriors all painted up " to beat the band,"
and their news was to the effect that they had seen
an enormous bull, who could only hold up his head
with difficulty on account of the abnormal weight
of his tusks.   Imagination ran riot on this elephant,
the only difficulty being that it was at a distance of
twelve miles away.   Nothing daunted by the
distance, I agreed to leave next morning very early
and go and shoot him, which, however, was not to
be.

That evening I arranged a little food, blanket, and
water-bottle filled with cold tea, and the next day I
set off, leaving the camp at 5 a.m.   Covering the
distance occupied nearly four hours, and I eagerly
scanned the valley in which the place was pointed
out to me as where this prince of bulls had lived
for the past week.   The warriors—or liars—even
pointed out to me the tree where he had stood the
day previous.   I then went down to the spot to see
what sort of a grip of Africa this bull possessed.
Arriving at the place, I failed to find any mark at
all—there had been no elephant there, and on
looking round for the two informants saw them

both clearing over the next ridge. They knew I had found out the truth and here was another twelve miles tramp back to camp, disappointed.

It is in situations as this, when you have been deliberately misled, that elephant hunting is not sport. Many of our African tribes are given to untruthfulness, which seems part of their religion and their second nature when buying or selling an ox, sheep or goat. If you give him the price asked, he is not satisfied, and prefers to argue the matter out for an hour at least, even bringing his forbears and ancestors into the deal.

I was tired out that night when I arrived back, and swore all the oaths remaining never to lend ear to them again, but after a night's rest and the disappointment wears off, you find some of them do tell tales with some particles of truth in them.

A " Dead " Elephant Departs

TWO days later, I found myself overlooking the western side of this plateau. Elephants were scattered about in several directions and I saw a single bull walking along the side of the hill towards a small hollow or crater. Hurrying along, I was watching him, expecting the animal to leave by walking through it. Not so. I arrived above this small crater, which was heavily bushed, and sat on a stone until he should show himself. My two natives sat beside me and eventually we saw the tops of the bushes swaying about, and here was a wonderful opportunity to shoot him in all safety, absolutely no risk, because we were sitting on high ground above him. Eventually his head appeared, just peering over the bushes, and I saw his tusks; they were very symmetrical and over the 70-lb. mark. He stood like this for a few minutes, taking off the top shoots with the tip of his trunk, and it was amusing to watch. His tummy rumbled, his ears swayed in front of him, never still, and then he moved sideways. Now, shooting downhill is always deceptive, as you are so apt to shoot high and miss the spot aimed at. I thought I would risk it, and aimed from a sitting position at his ear. He dropped to my shot instanter and fell on his side. The two natives, in their way of expressing pleasure,

patted me on the back for my wonderful shot. I
watched that elephant lying there for several
minutes and sent off one of the boys to bring a
chopper from the camp to cut out his tusks.

The other native, in the meantime, saw several
more elephants ahead of me which were standing
close together, and off we went to bag a second one
in the first hour's hunting. When at least 100
yards from this small herd, a bull, carrying only
50 lb. of ivory in each tusk, charged straight in my
direction, with ears extended and trunk lowered,
tucked into his brisket. He certainly looked the
essence of danger. This was too much for my
native, who fled barefooted over that broken ground
as if he were running on sand. The elephant
stopped within forty yards in front of me, and then
doubled back to the herd and carried out the same
procedure on the opposite side. He was evidently
out to protect that herd, which was mostly composed
of cows, and I thought he had heard the first shot
at the elephant in the crater, suspected danger, and
had just attacked at nothing, expecting to find
something. When this bull rejoined the herd, they
all moved away, but the way they kept huddled together proved they knew mankind, their only
enemy, was hovering near them, and in that open
ground they were practically at his mercy.

In the meantime, the native I had sent for the
chopper had returned, together with the cook in a
clean, white kanzu or dress. He wanted his picture
taken beside an elephant to show his friends that he
was a man of the forest. On approaching the small

crater, the boys commenced a chant, which, however, was curtailed, not by the elephant, but by his
absence.   I had handed over my heavy rifle to one
of the boys, and as we drew near to the place where
my elephant fell, these boys bolted back as if a herd
of elephant was after them.   It was useless to try
and stop them, they would not have heard.   Now,
being empty-handed, I wished myself at some other
place also.

It did not add to the enjoyment when a water-
buck crashed out within a few yards of me.   Did I
feel my hair stand on end ?   Emphatically yes !
Retrieving my rifle, I then cautiously approached
and inspected.   There was the flattened ground
where that elephant had lain on his side; there was
the mark of one tusk which had ploughed into the
hard earth when he fell; there were the droppings
which are always a certain sign that death has overtaken him—and my elephant gone.   There was
congealed blood where he had lain, and I followed
the spoor through the bush.   He had simply
vanished and had beat it for the forest in the valley
below, which was nearly half a mile away.   I then
realised that when the other elephant charged back
at me from the herd, he had heard some sound from
my supposedly dead elephant.   I followed on this
spoor, and in the heavy bush it became mixed up
with other marks of elephants which were in the
same vicinity, and to make matters worse a heavy
thunderstorm burst over me, and this made the
tracks quite impossible.   I knew that should he die
in that forest, hyænas would soon give me the cue

as to where his carcase lay, as within three days they will make distinct tracks to a decomposed animal.

This elephant was never recovered, and it often happens that the head shot, without penetrating the brain, means an elephant lost. That is why I now advocate the shoulder shot, if the position of the head does not offer you the brain. My shot evidently passed close to the brain, rendering the animal unconscious. As a rule, if you do not get the brain correctly, they fall down, but only moment-arily, and are up in a fraction of a minute, but to stay down for several minutes is exceptional. Probably my grief was less than that of the sports-man who shot an elephant in the late evening, actually cut off the tail, and on going next morning for his tusks found his elephant had disappeared without his rudder !

The natives' love for elephant meat in that sector south of Lake Victoria was really past understand-ing. When I have been approaching elephant in the open country, my attention has been drawn to the number of black specks on the hilltops—just like crows—all waiting to hear the sound of a rifle. On one occasion a bull was shot, and being shot in the brain, died on its knees. The natives were soon on the scene and knives of all shapes and sizes were soon being sharpened on the rough stones near by. At a given word they were all into the carcase, cutting and tearing and acting as savages proper, many of them even eating the meat in its raw state. Cutting into the flank, three of them, quite naked, pulled out the intestines and actually

c

entered the carcase—fat round the heart was the attraction—and it was not long before the noise these three savages made inside that elephant was equal to that of any fighting dogs. One of them came out, a bloody mess, with his hand cut by the others' knives. They had actually been cutting at each other inside the carcase.

On another occasion four elephants were killed in close proximity to each other and in twenty-four hours every scrap of meat was gone, and the reason for these natives leaving their long spears in a circle beside the bones is probably connected with witchcraft, with which I am not yet acquainted.

I hunted in this area for nearly eighteen months and saw many elephants shot—at this period there were approximately three thousand of them roaming in an area of sixty square miles. The country generally on this plateau was open, ideal and easy for the beginner. In the valleys below it was different, being heavily timbered and in parts infested with tsetse fly, the bite of which is fatal to cattle, but harmless though aggravating to man. It was in one of these wooded belts that I followed up a single bull which eventually took me straight into an enormous herd of elephants, comprised of animals of all sizes. I had just dodged one lot when a cow elephant passed me, carrying a thick branch of a tree in her mouth. It reminded me of someone I knew who held his pipe at a peculiar angle.

Things became too hot for me in this forest, known as Berwa, where the natives informed me that elephant cows gave birth to their young. Scuttling up a tree, I had a wonderful sight; little ones sucked by their mothers; the tips of branches continually held aloft, testing the wind and throwing dust and red earth over their backs. I have even seen them, when hot and after running for some distance, cooling themselves with a spray of water, ejected through the trunk from their innards.

My large elephant disappeared entirely from me, as with so many scattered over the forest it was quite impossible to get near him without disturbing others.

It was in similar type of country one day, when I accompanied a sportsman bent on shooting an elephant, that we came across two bulls, one good and the other poor. It is surprising, but when in thick bush, the latter will always present you with an easy shot, the larger one not so. And again, the smaller one always appears to get in your way. Following these bulls into thick bush, which was very dense, in parts intermixed with wild sisal, and moving in the tracks of these beasts meant many painful stabs, we crept on, moving very cautiously, and we could hear them feeding, the rumble of their intestines occurring every ten minutes or so throughout the day. They appeared to be standing some thirty yards apart, but on account of the density of the bush it was quite impossible to see them at more than five yards. Standing listening, or watching through the lower undergrowth, seems to take up much time, while you are ever waiting to get a glimpse of the bull carrying the long, thick tusks. A heavy branch was broken in front of us. That must be the big one, we thought, and moved quietly on, barely missing the sharp-pointed, poisonous sisal tips. We saw the dark mass standing amidst the green foliage, and moved a yard forward —the bush is so thick you can only walk in Indian file. The beast caught the sound and came forward; in two steps he was practically above us. It was the small tusker and we could not get away from him; it would have been suicidal. I did the only alternative, which was to shoot, the bullet hitting him in the roof of the mouth, reaching the brain, and he crashed. We then had the satisfaction —or otherwise—of hearing the animal we were after tearing off through the bush, to live and be hunted another day by someone else.

It may not be generally known that when the elephant does kill a human being, his anger, his hatred, is so violent that, apart from mangling you with foot, trunk and tusk, he will break branches off the trees near and pile them on you to hide you from his gaze. Even the natives, with all their fleetness and climbing powers—akin to the monkey —do not always get away, and these poachers have informed me that when the elephant hears the twang of the bow he will double back in anger, trying to find the cause, and if they are caught up a tree, this will be pulled down and the natives killed.

In parts of the Congo Belge, in the lower Ituri forest, there is a tribe living near a chain of large salt licks who actually spear elephants, getting alongside of them and holding their spears in front at an angle, when the elephant charges. He charges and spears himself.

Wishing to scout in this tsetse fly area, I proceeded to a rocky kopje, at the foot of which was a small spring of good water. Right on the summit I discovered a regular poachers' den, bushed up and completely hidden from anyone below. It had not been occupied for probably a month, and here I thought I would remain for at least three days. In the semi-open bush below I could plainly see roan antelope and topi. At five o'clock that evening a considerable herd of elephants was seen about a mile off, coming straight for the hill I was perched on. They appeared to be coming from the direction of the Gori river, where it enters Lake Victoria, and trekking eastwards to the Utendi district. This herd comprised over a hundred elephants, and on coming to the hill they divided and circled round. When they picked up the scent of my safari they seemed to go crazy and tore round that hill for some minutes, which appeared much longer, while the position looked unsatisfactory. As long as the elephants faced the summit there was not a sound in the camp, but immediately they turned and moved away the boys yelled and yodelled and those elephants tore off, the bushes and undergrowth being pulled out in their mad stampede. Knowing that no other elephants would stay or settle in a place marked by this wild, flying mob, we moved the camp next morning, having drawn a blank at a place which otherwise should have been good.

I was hunting later in company with another, and amongst the other animals required on our list were four elephants. The border of a Game Reserve was the chosen spot, hoping for the ever unobtainable to cross over the demarcated line. In the first two days we were unsuccessful with elephants, but shot a very good rhino. On the third day a herd of elephants was spotted from the top of a rocky hill which dominated the bush below. I was surprised to see the number of scorpions lying dead on the top of the hill, each having the tail or poison sting torn off—good work done by baboons. That these animals kill countless numbers of these pests is undoubted.

We watched these elephants until they were in bush to our liking, descended and had no difficulty in getting up to them. My friend found an ideal spot, where he waited and they simply filed past him, when he dropped the best, which was the rear one, with a clean shot through the back of the head. The other animals were surprised, but just continued slowly on. Following them, while crossing some open bush, my friend picked up the spoor of a large bull elephant which had passed early that morning; it was heading north and we followed on and on, actually covering about ten miles.

Now we were quite unprepared to stay out the night, having no food or water, and the day can be cruelly hot. At 5 p.m. we came across a muddy pool where he had drunk and from this mess we drank also. It is surprising what you will drink if compelled.

Within a mile we heard him in a piece of Africa's
worst country composed of " wait-a-bit " thorn,
intermixed with sansiviera or wild sisal. The
only trail to follow was his, and the prods in our
legs and pants were anything but encouraging.
To cut a long story short, I could now see the outline
of this elephant. He looked lean, his backbone
highly ridged, and while manœuvring to get a
shot he heard me and crashed on. He stopped a
few hundred yards distant and we followed. Now
it is not so bad picking your way in any bush,
providing you do not have the African nettle or
sisal to hamper your movements. Here were
both and, moreover, a disturbed and listening
elephant in front. Dark was now coming on and
I hoped we would yet get him—consolation for
a night in the bush without food or water. Creeping cautiously, my friend was splendid; I could
not hear him. I perceived something black in the
bush in front of me. We stopped and looked;
it was part of his trunk, the only part of that six-ton
mass, standing so still in front of us, that we could
see. I tried my best to see a suitable place to shoot
at, and had I been six feet high might have accomplished it. I could hear my friend remarking,
" For God's sake, Hunter, put in a good shot."
I wanted to do the next best thing, which was to
fire where I thought his head would be. At
my shot he rushed forward, and my friend did not
await closer acquaintance—and I do not blame
him—but cut into the right, without getting a
sisal stab in the act. Had I done this, I could

not have missed it. The next moment I heard a shot near me and the elephant crashed off. Joining up, we decided to sleep where we were and as we were, and follow up the bull in the morning as soon as daylight would permit. That night was a most uncomfortable one, our bed being hard mother earth. The pangs of hunger wore off and next morning we continued our hunt.

Following the spoor, we could see where he had stopped and turned, facing the direction we would come. There was a certain amount of blood spoor, but from the colour it was evident he was hit too far back by my friend and not well enough forward by me. It was a disappointment when we found that he had passed through this bush and continued across open country, heading for the Game Reserve, some five miles distant. We simply could not lose him, and our only hope lay in cutting to the Game Reserve and making a big circle, hoping that we could intercept him—which actually did happen. Making a big flanking movement, we discovered a well-used rhino trail which was evidently leading to water. Following this for a mile, we actually came on five rhinos, all lying down for the day, their twitching ears being the only sign of movement. We had no wish to disturb them, lest they would crash and maybe scare the elephant. We circled round them and found the path again, eventually coming up to a beautiful clear spring. This was a joy after the filth we had imbibed the previous afternoon. To the left of us was a heavy belt of forest, but luckily no sisal. We had seen no tracks of the elephant leading out, so we still had some hope of seeing him. Taking it slowly with the wind in our favour, one of our boys heard a noise ahead of us and said "migu" (Swahili word for baboon). My friend, not satisfied, suggested waiting and then we heard another branch break.

We were satisfied it was our elephant heading straight for us. We waited there for the brave beast which had charged us in his own ground the previous night, made us give way, and now the tide had turned in our favour; we could move and manœuvre. It did not take him long to come. He was making use of the best cover available, and then he stopped. Did his instinct tell him that danger was beside him as he stopped, looking and listening, yet the wind was against him? He was ambushed. His sides appeared thin and he faced us to die as he was, a brave beast. His tusks weighed 90 lb. each, a splendid pair. My shot from the previous evening had only glanced from his skull owing to the angle at which he was standing, doing practically no damage.

We made our way back to the camp, hungry and tired, yet satisfied and pleased that we had not left a wounded elephant behind.

More Elephant

SOME ten years ago I accompanied three sportsmen who came to Kenya to hunt big game, and the bag could not be complete without an elephant. The area chosen was east of Kitui, an outpost in Kenya situated east of the Athi river. Local natives informed us of a good bull which had been doing considerable damage to their shambas, or crops, for some time, and were overjoyed to think that the marauder would be slain.

At camp that night an Ngoma or native dance was staged in their honour, the dancers mainly consisting of young native girls, decorated with beads, blowing police whistles in unison. The rumba part of it, at which these girls excel, was great, and our hearts were light for the morrow. These sportsmen cross-examined the local talent as to the length of the tusks this elephant carried, and had this been persisted in it is doubtful as to what length or dimensions they would have grown.

Sending our local guides to visit certain water-holes where this elephant drank, news came back that he had visited there early that morning. Now here was one elephant and three keen sportsmen, all bent on slaying him. They tossed as to who should shoot first, and even that did not prove satisfactory.

Following his spoor, the noise they made was appalling, and I was not surprised that the native guide kept looking back in disgust. This was something new to his silent way of stalking or following. The tracks of the elephant led us into thick cover, the bushes being covered with creeping vines from which, when broken, oozed a milky fluid. After two hours' trailing the native heard the elephant and asked me to request the party, all so eager and keen, to go quietly. It was useless. They were silent for a few yards and then came the inevitable crashing through, which even a partly deaf elephant could have heard.

Near a swampy portion the elephant screamed, and then there was a commotion. The tallest of the party, who I never dreamt or believed could climb, was up a tree and bawling at the top of his voice: " I can see him. Give me a rifle." The position for the other two down below was not so good, and their expressions did not deny the fact. My friend on the tree with his ·470 fired. I am sure he pulled both triggers together, and the result was he lost his balance and came down even quicker than he went up. In the meantime, the elephant, with the terrible din, had cleared off, little hurt but much frightened by the incident. That was the last we saw of the elephant, and I was not surprised when one of the other two elephant shooters complained of bunions and decided to return to camp and hunt elephants another day. This hunt proved a failure, but it was against all the rules and instincts which govern hunting.

From the charges I have witnessed I should say that the speed attained by an infuriated elephant would reach twenty miles an hour, and this could be maintained for at least 150 yards.

In trekking from one district to another their normal speed would reach ten miles an hour.

The next hunt with this party proved more fruitful. We moved from this part of the colony to a quiet, undisturbed corner in the Northern Frontier Province where elephants, rhino, and many varieties of antelopes were plentiful. We made our camp near a stream forty miles south of Meru on the old military route, long since closed, which led to Garbatulla. The roads here were appalling, and with recent rains transport was most difficult. One of our lorries had not arrived with the safari and I returned to look for it, finding it bogged near Nanyuki.

On arriving at camp the following day at noon with the missing lorry, I was met by my friend the elephant shot, who, in great glee, informed me that he had seen a rhino and shot it up properly. On my asking to see the horns, he said he had not inspected them, but would show me where they lay. Within half a mile of the camp he pointed to a tree, and on arrival sure enough, from the empty cartridge shells underneath, there had been much shooting done. Approaching with caution the clump of brush where the rhino was last seen, I heard a snort and a noise like escaping steam, and out came the rhino straight for us, charging all out. It was shot at close quarters, my friend remarking,

" It cannot be the same one," but from its previous marks there was no doubt as to its identity. I would add here that the horns this beast carried were among the poorest I had yet seen.

Moving camp further south, we hunted elephants. On account of the sandy soil and the sparse bush, the going was easier. Walking leisurely along the river, a lesser kudu jumped up and my friend took it on the run, a neat shot.

While discussing the chance of elephants we heard the noise of one at least half a mile away. The report of the single shot at the kudu had not disturbed him. It seldom does; it is only with the sound of the second or third shot they become alarmed. It is extraordinary how elephants can differentiate between sounds—namely, the sharp rattling peals of thunder and the report of a rifle which spells death. I have watched these huge beasts wandering about in a heavy thunderstorm with the deafening cracks overhead, taking not the slightest notice, and yet a few shots fired in the same area and they are off to seek " pastures new."

In the animal kingdom the same will apply to those wily animals, the lion and the bongo. That animals have a sense of communication is beyond doubt, because when aware of the presence of danger they will entirely leave the area within three days' hunting. Therefore your best chances of success are within this period. This all boils down to a matter of wits 'twixt cunning men and savage beasts.

Speaking of wits, a friend of mine owned a

baboon, a species I detest. In some ways this animal appeared human and understanding. He even liked his tobacco, and to see him hold a pipe in his mouth was too ridiculous. This was somewhat marred by his lack of intelligence, as I will describe.

The baboon, like all monkeys, was very partial to bananas. A bunch of this fruit was suspended by a cord to the ceiling, and empty petrol boxes piled up where he could ascend to reach the bananas. This he immediately did. The owner removing two of the empty cases, the baboon, on going up again, could not understand being unable to reach. The fact that he did not think of replacing the boxes showed his grey matter did not tell him to use his hands.

I must apologise to my readers for leaving my narrative. Continuing towards the place where the sound emanated, the outline of a single bull was seen slowly feeding in an open part of the bush, quite unsuspecting of the array awaiting him. Moving up to him was easy work, and there he stood facing us. A heavy rifle spoke, and the bullet hit him between the eyes and he dropped in one movement—surely a humane ending to a long career.

It may interest many of my readers to learn that I am of the opinion these magnificent animals live to the great age of 150 years; even the average bull carrying 60 lb. of ivory in each tusk has taken half a century to produce them. The period of gestation in these huge pachyderms is roughly twenty months, and shooting these animals to some may appear a stupendous crime. A giant beast that has roamed in the African bush for a century and a half can be destroyed in a split fraction by that deadly missile of death, the bullet. Throughout these years they are ever on the alert against their only enemy, mankind, and it is really surprising how they have held their own against the pitfalls of savagedom and the weapons of modern civilisation.

Up to a few years ago the price of their coveted tusks told heavily against them, but now science and art in fine enamel has in fashion's path replaced the heavy ivory as of old.

Elephant cemeteries have been mentioned where old bulls, feeling their days numbered, were wont to trek and die. Personally, I do not hold with this belief, and it may be dismissed as a myth. Fourteen years ago I was hunting in mountainous country and a large collection of elephant bones was shown to me under a precipitous cliff, where I am sure there were the remains of at least thirty of these fine beasts. I was much interested, and on making full enquiries was informed by the local natives the cause of this elephant cemetery. An entire herd of these fine animals during the rains had wandered out of their usual course and were chased and hounded by a mob of yelling natives with dogs. The elephants entirely lost their direction and, finding themselves on the brink of a precipice, one of them either slipped over or took the plunge, but, sad to relate, the remainder followed, taking a drop of 200 feet. Their tusks were actually gathered in splinters, sacks being used to carry them. The reader can imagine the indescribable and dreadful mangled mess depicted, which—thank the powers that be today—could not recur.

On my first trip hunting elephants in the Liwali and Mahenge districts of Tanganyika, the Game Warden, Captain Fairweather, then in charge of the elephant control scheme, kindly loaned me one of his best native scouts to show me those parts. This scout was engaged in shooting elephants which were doing damage to the native crops (but then most elephants do). He was certainly one of the best native hunters I have ever seen. His rifle was a ·404 Jeffry Mauser, and his average bag was upwards of thirty elephants monthly. When he came to me, he had just had an alarming encounter with a wounded bull, and declared he would treat these animals with more respect onwards. His clothes were torn from the effects, and I asked him to tell me what happened, which I will now relate.

He followed the spoor of a bull from an outlying maize field and came up with him standing amongst some wild rubber saplings, a distance of three miles from where he had fed. Approaching to within fifteen yards of the elephant, he fired behind its shoulder, which it acknowledged with a groan, and before he realised, the elephant was on top of him, standing screaming, while it was doing its best to spit him on its tusks, jabbing them into the ground on either side of him. He managed to crawl back between the fore-legs and lay flat under the belly, while it kept kicking its hind feet fore and aft, one of its feet knocking off his old felt hat, which it promptly put its tusk through. While engaged on the hat, he managed to crawl out, and in its terrible fury it had soaked him with urine as he had lain there. Recovering his rifle, he hastily fired a shot into the orifice of its ear, and it dropped dead. Now this native had shot hundreds of elephants, and here was the only one which gave trouble, and it was only by a miracle that he escaped.

To say the least of it, elephants are dainty feeders, and it is surprising to see how they discriminate in selecting their food, choosing shoots from individual trees and branches, and feeding by night time, mostly by sense of smell, refusing to eat from the majority of our forest bush. I have watched them place their mighty forehead or the point of their shoulder against the trunk of a tree, up to two feet in diameter, and put their colossal weight, up to six tons, against it, using a swaying motion, which usually brings it down within five minutes. They then proceed to eat the shoots from the uppermost branches.

Their methods of negotiating steep banks up to twenty feet is most interesting. I have seen them, where the banks lie at an angle of forty-five degrees, stretching their forelegs and taking the slide on their hunkers. It is indeed surprising to see how quickly they can perform this feat, the dust raised from the sandbanks usually more or less obscuring them. Elephants in some ways are handicapped, as they cannot, like most of the other animals,

D

jump or gallop.   Should he come to a steep ravine
where the walls are perpendicular, he has no option
but to go round if the distance is beyond his stride.
I am of the opinion that he would not negotiate
such a width exceeding six feet, and here lies one's
safety in jumping, if ever such a predicament
occurred.

Having hunted and shot elephants in five different
countries in Africa, I have seen enormous numbers,
and it is my opinion that those in Eastern Africa
are more prone to attack and " lose their rag "
than in the Congo and Central.   In the latter
places I took liberties with elephants in the vast
Ituri Forest which I certainly could not with those
in the Northern Frontier Province in Kenya.

It may interest the reader to know that there is
an elephant farm in the Belgian Congo where
elephants are trained and have become useful
adjuncts to civilisation.   I am doubtful if this could
ever be applicable to our East African elephant,
imbued with his blind untamable fury.   In times
of distress I have heard of elephants assisting one
another, bolstering a wounded one along, and so
forth, but in all my wanderings I have never seen
any such assistance offered, and am inclined to
think that the elephant too frail or injured to continue would be left to his own resources.   That
elephants will stand by a fallen one is well known,
but this can only be as a rule attributed to clean
shooting on the part of the hunter and quietness
after doing so.

In the South Meru districts along the slopes of

the Ngai hills there were many wide and deep
elephant trails worn down by these great beasts
during centuries past, even the rocks in some places
being caved out by the action of their hard soles.
This was a much favoured spot for the elephant
hunter, and I well remember seeing a native digging
in his maize patch, and noticing the spoor of several
elephants having passed through that morning.
As it was late in the evening, I decided to stay there,
and noticed a small hut built up in the fork of a
substantial tree. I was again without food or
blanket, and as I wished to be on the spot by
daybreak, decided to make my home for the night
in that pigeon-like coop. I managed to get a few
green bananas from the old native digging in his
shamba and took up a supply of branches which
I could pile over me for weight, if not warmth.
The night was indeed cold and in the early hours
I shivered. During the night I heard elephants
passing through the bush under me, the noise of
them brushing through the bush being similar
to that produced by gushing wind, but on account
of the darkness it was quite impossible to distinguish
what size they were. I dozed off and was awakened
by the bark of a bush buck.

As soon as it was light enough to see spoor I
climbed down, and here I was ready to follow up
anything good. Passing through the shamba, I
soon picked up the trail of several bulls heading
towards the recesses of Ngai Hill. In the first
mile I came across a solitary bull, standing like a
sentinel of the African bush. He offered an easy

shot and I continued on to look for another, as I noticed that at least five bulls had passed in the night. Coming over a ridge there were four more, walking slowly and feeding as they went. One of the bulls was outstanding, showing six feet of ivory from the lip. Here was my bull, but he was some distance in front; getting above them meant everything in my favour. I actually managed to get ahead of them and waited near a dry watercourse. When he came parallel with me I fired, shooting him in the point of the shoulder, and then gave him a second shot behind. He stood beaten, swayed and fell. The tusks weighed out at 90 and 94 lb. Now here were two fine bulls shot within one hour's hunting, and made easy by my sleeping under discomfort for one night. Had my camp been near this locality, they would have been disturbed either by the smell of fires or by noise, and taken unnecessary time to secure.

Shot down before an Elephant

ON one occasion I had trekked for hours under a broiling sun, and the heat at midday can be treacherous. I had a spare water-bottle with me in case of emergency and I saw in the distance a bunch of bulls standing in shade about a mile in front of me. Having already finished my first bottle, I called for the second, and imagine my disgust when I found it empty—one of the natives following me had drunk the lot. It is probably the feeling of no water with you which makes your thirst all the keener and harder. Your lips become dry and parched and your throat cracks. I have suffered from thirst, and, believe me, hunger cannot be compared with it.

Grass fires were in progress all over the district to the west of me in the direction of the Tana River, and I saw some smoke on the off-side of the bunch of elephants. I watched the elephants putting up their trunks in the direction of the smoke, and then they all moved up the hill, passing half a mile in front of me. I went to try and intercept them. There were at least three good ones, and here is one of the times when I was entirely beaten by thirst. The spirit was willing, but I could not do it. It is a terrible feeling, and unless you have experienced it, it is even difficult to imagine. As it was, I had to turn back and waited until the late afternoon, when I retraced my steps downhill towards camp. On my way back I suffered, and I even thought of all the water taps I had passed in my life and had not partaken of water from them.

Even elephants in many parts of the Northern Frontier Province have been brought down to more or less poor creatures—capable of little danger —when reduced to this stage by thirst and insufficient feeding. I remember, when passing a water-hole where Somalis used to dig for water in the bed of a dry river, finding that an elephant cow and calf appeared in the early hours of the morning and pulled a native up from the well with her trunk while thus engaged in digging, killing him instantly.

In the colder climates and when not exposed to much of the tropical sun, elephants may only drink once every second day, but during the hottest weather when most of their shelter has gone and the leaves have lost their sap, they will drink daily, usually each evening, the cows coming first and the lone bull or company later.

Elephants and buffalo often live together in the same locality, and do not mind each other's presence. When hunting elephant, I have seen buffalo feeding near them, and it is best to let the buffalo continue on their way if possible, otherwise they will gallop off and stampede the elephants, entirely spoiling your measure of success.

That all the animals have some form of communication is beyond doubt. A strange and interesting sight happened one day in open bush country

where a party had crossed an hour or so previously.
The elephants—about fifteen of them—stopped
dead on the spoor of the safari and two of the cows
actually put their trunks down on the spoor, joined
them together, and the herd doubled back in alarm.

It is distinctly unnerving to find yourself in the
midst of a herd of elephants feeding in bush, as
they appear to cover the ground so quickly, en-
circling you before you realise it. I have always
found it easier to get in than to get out. The
noise of their pushing through the dense foliage,
coupled with breaking heavy branches, fills the
atmosphere with awe. Even the snake, quickly
gliding away to a safe distance in front, alarmed
by the fearsome noise, will give thrills where others
fail. Matters are at times liable to take an alarming
complex, especially if the surrounding bush is of
the treacherous " wait-a-bit " thorn variety, armed
with its formidable hook-like thorns which ensnare
you from any angle. The Voi district in Kenya
excels in this horrible thorn-set bush.

Elephants are very partial to the large bulbous
roots found all over the sandy desert country, and
it is surprising how they know where to dig in the
ground with their tusks even to a depth of three
feet to secure them. The right tusk is generally
used for digging out roots and bulbs, and in consequence this tusk is prone to get worn down or even
broken. In some parts I have seen both tusks
deeply ridged all round within six inches from the
tip, evidently caused by a screwing or twisting
motion while digging in the harder grounds.

Shot down before an elephant—and yet that happened to me not many years ago. I was hunting with a party and my host was a great and safe sportsman. Big bulls were the order of the day, and this party was indeed lucky, securing three of them in so many days, and all practically in the 100 lb. per tusk margin. Now in the dry weather, the large bulls and others are all compelled to drink near the larger streams on account of the smaller ones and water-holes drying up. During the heavy rains there are many parts throughout the desert which hold water for many months, and while there is water there the elephants feed in the surrounding area.

For three months of the year elephant hunting is then comparatively easy, and by seeing the spoor you can get a good idea as to the number of elephants in the locality. In fact, I believe that by this method a fairly complete census could be taken. During this period they lie up within ten miles from the river, or even half this distance. There they will stand on a ridge getting any breeze blowing, heads facing the wind. On several occasions I have seen elephant and native cattle all standing by the same water-hole. They love to stand in the water up to their stomach and throw water all over themselves. In Lake Albert I have actually seen them practically submerged. That they are powerful swimmers there is no doubt, and they can cover half a mile with ease.

On one occasion I saw one of them shot on the edge of a lake and the carcase floated immediately, half the body visible on the surface, on account of its buoyancy.

When in the lake it is most interesting to get a canoe and paddle slowly out beyond them and watch their love for water. They splash and thoroughly enjoy themselves. Crocodiles are numerous on the shores of this lake where the elephants bathe, but I have never seen one attacked, although I was informed by a friend of mine who was shooting elephants near the Rufigi river in Tanganyika that he actually saw a crocodile dragged out by an elephant, which was hanging on to the hind leg. When the elephant reached the bank it seized it with its trunk and smashed it on to the ground. There probably are many similar cases which never come to light.

Returning to my narrative, this party, including myself, were down in a district where even today ivory weighs heavy and the 100-lb. tusker is not infrequently met with. In fact, there are still many of them. Proceeding down a track within three miles of the camp, several elephant were seen, and we passed them up, as the ivory was not heavy enough for " mine host's " liking.

Finding the spoor of some more, a little further on, we followed them, and here was a fine mob of fifteen bulls. Two were outstanding—one had long tusks, about eight feet of ivory showing, but not as thick as his confrere. The former was the finest trophy, but the tusks would not exceed 90 lb. each, so we selected the latter. The sportsman in this instance was a born hunter. He walked with the stealth of a panther, and was careful in passing bush. In fact, you did not know he was behind you and yet he was always ready to rush in when necessary. He was followed by a personal attendant who was carrying a second rifle. Approaching that bull to within fifteen yards, he took a quick aim and fired—the elephant falling instantly. So much for our first, and the second bull was also secured on the following day under much the same conditions. This will give the observer or reader an idea as to the precaution required in elephant hunting. Quietness and a steady wind in your favour are the two dominating factors.

On the third day—it was nearly my unlucky one—we hunted a few miles further inland and some native scouts brought news of elephant within a mile of the main road. They informed us that there were many, but could not see what weight of tusks they carried. We followed along to investigate and spotted a bull standing with his head lowered amongst some thick undergrowth. Here was an easy shoulder shot at fifty yards, but only one tusk was visible and it is so easy in bush to shoot a single tusker, which we wanted to avoid. After watching him for some time he moved away and then it was seen he carried his pair. We would have followed him, but on account of a small herd on his left, which we did not wish to disturb, were forced to make a circuit to avoid them getting our wind. Had they done so, they would have cleared.

We did not have to walk far before noticing our

bull coming in a straight line towards us. Waiting until he was within twenty yards range, I pointed between his eyes, and my sportsman hit him square, using a double Express Holland ·475 No. 2, which simply pushed him back on his haunches. At this time, I really forget, someone let off a heavy rifle by accident behind me, the blast of the charges passing my ear—too near—and the shock put me down, I was informed at the same time as the elephant—hunter and elephant down at the same report! I had the unbosomed feeling of intense relief, finding myself wafted into space with utmost ease, and everything appeared bright and peaceful. Then I came to my senses with the voice of my faithful gun bearer arguing with everyone as to why it happened!

There may be many sportsmen who are under the impression that these magnificent elephants carrying over 200 lb. weight in ivory do not exist today, but I say, without fear of contradiction, there are many of them carrying far above this weight, but, alas! the big majority are only to be found in Kenya Colony.

Even with all these shortcomings, I am sure many will agree with me that elephant hunting is still the finest sport in the world. It is thrilling, and in years to come will find the same appeal to many as to those wonderful sportsmen of the past.

Encounters with the King of Beasts

LIONS—the name inspires—are found over most of Africa, even today. Certainly where civilisation has moved apace, so have these big members of the cat family been compelled to retreat against the forces of mankind. Where they have been hunted a great deal they confine themselves to the bush and are seldom seen in the day, only prowling out under cover of darkness, and returning at early dawn.

In other parts, especially Eastern Africa, where they are still to be seen in considerable numbers, they seldom lie up in cover, preferring the fringes of our vast plains, which literally teem with game. In many of these plains a rough estimate of animals to be seen in one day would be about six thousand.

Without any question of doubt, Tanganyika territory (formerly German East Africa, and now Mandated Territory) holds the bulk of the lions in Africa. The vast Serengeti plains and adjoining areas are splendid and ideal lion country.

What makes it the more interesting is that this full show of game does not come under a Game Reserve. It is not infrequent to see up to fifty lions, both sexes, in one day. I have actually seen twenty-seven in one pride, although troops of fifteen are common. The lioness usually has cubs in April, the average litter being three, although four are not uncommon. The lioness usually has her litter amongst rocky ground, being partial to the cavities underneath. When the cubs are about ten days old, the mother will bring small antelopes beside the cubs and they will lick the blood and get their first initiation to the taste for meat.

Rickets are the cause of a big mortality amongst cubs; this is probably due to eating meat while too young to digest it.

The weight of a fully grown lion is 450 lb. He is able to drag an animal double his own weight, the procedure being to catch it behind the ear, dragging it and putting it down at intervals of fifteen yards or so until he reaches the nearest cover. In killing the larger animals they usually spring on the withers or neck of the beast and turn the head, causing it to stumble, and in falling breaking its neck, the lion making doubly sure by biting it in the break.

Lions are in the habit of drinking every night between 7 and 10 p.m., and again in the early hours of the morning if they have killed and fed. Should a pride be in possession of the kill, they will not all proceed to drink at the same time, part of the number remaining to guard it from hyænas and other vermin. Lions do not mind jackals approaching their bait, but will charge at hyænas should they come too close for their liking. When lions roar—and one hears them so seldom—it is a wonderfully awe-inspiring sound; the very ground seems to tremble.

I remember in 1910 when a pride of lions came to drink at a certain underground water tank. Its aperture was covered with a corrugated iron sheet on which was placed a heavy weight. Finding their access barred, they commenced roaring, and the concert from these three males was deafening and reverberating. They were really grand to behold, and it is probably from their majestic notes that the King of Beasts found his title. In the game areas today, where there are hundreds of lions, you may not hear even one roar in the course of a week—only the low hunting grunts or calls. I have accompanied many visitors all keen and anxious to hear a lion roar, and lucky is he who hears it. I have watched lion feed on zebra and other animals, and it is surprising what neat square chunks of meat they can take at each bite. They will actually gorge until their sides bulge out, the swaying stomach not adding to their dignity. They are then content to fast for the next three days. Lions do not as a rule kill daily, but they will take bait if dragged to them, especially if the diet be changed, say, from zebra, wildebeeste and hartebeeste. The colder climates as a rule furnish the best black-maned lions, and some of the best specimens I know were shot on the slopes of Kilimanjaro, Lolikisali in Tanganyika, and the Mau in Kenya. I do not believe in the theory that lions are monogamists, but with the leopard I find it is so.

Man-eating lions—in darkness fearsome, hellish beasts, whose daring and determination know no bounds—are the most dreaded in Africa and certainly to be feared.

In many parts today several of our African tribes do not trouble to bury their dead. The dead, and the very sick, are often taken from their kraals and placed in the bush some distance away, to be actually taken away by wild animals; hyænas and lions being the scavengers. It is a terrible admission to make, but nevertheless true. Owing to the big native population in some areas, one might expect to find human bones all over the place, but this is not so.

At times when I have been hunting, in heavy bush, far from the ordinary hunting routes, I have found the burrows of antbears occupied by hyænas, the place littered with human bones ghastly toothless skulls adding to the horror.

Now there may be times when no dead bodies can be found and the lion, once having tasted human flesh and hungry, will actually kill, which is only natural for him to do—hence my theory.

When natives are made to realise that their dead must be properly interred, then I am sure the man-eating menace will fizzle out. When I was actually hunting lions amongst a tribe whose methods were as described, I was requested by them not to shoot the hyænas on account of their assistance, and if a body was deposited on the bush and still there next morning, this was accepted as a curse on the part of his or her relations, and a goat or sheep had to be given up in consequence.

I am now going to describe to my readers a

number of personal experiences concerning hunting lions, and trust I will not be branded as a killer.
At the request of Government and others, I have
shot many which were doing a considerable amount
of damage to life and stock.   These, coupled with
numbers shot over a period of many years' hunting,
have amounted to more than several hundred, thus
covering the most of Eastern and Central Africa.
I have hunted them by every method: by foot,
tracking them to their dens, driving them from
ravines and swamps, stirring them out of bushes,
and even sitting beside bait for them, and I claim
to have had experiences seldom, if ever, equalled
by anyone in the annals of African hunting.   In
connection with lions, I never tried the plan of
sitting in a dug-out hole waiting for them, as the
sitting position in an all-night vigil did not appeal
to me.

The natives shoot lions with bow and arrow on
the Machan principle, and have been known to
kill several in a night, the arrow passing through
the animal and lodging against the skin on the off
side.   As their arrows are poisoned, being coated
with a preparation similar to bird lime, the lion
seldom goes more than 100 yards after being hit.
Apart from the wound, the paralysing properties
of the poison kill it.

When lions become very old and unable to kill
their own food, they usually fall victims to hyænas.
Now the flesh of lion or leopard to a hyæna is like
candy to a child.   Hyænas will laugh and chuckle
over the carcase of these animals more than over any

other meat I know. I remember sitting up for a leopard in a bush. At about 9 p.m. in the faint light of the moon, I saw it steal forward. Eventually coming on the carcase, I shot it. He died about ten yards from the kill and I made up my mind to sleep in the bush until morning, but before doing so I went to the leopard and by the use of his tail I pulled him up to within a few feet of where I lay, making it, as I thought, safe from the hyænas. I lost that leopard. I woke up in the early hours hearing a terrible commotion outside my hide: two hyænas had actually sneaked forward and snatched my dead leopard and were dragging it away. I went after them and those hyænas mocked me. I could hear them racing with it, chuckling, and in the semi-darkness I could not see them and had to let them have it, much against my will.

Hunting from Tsavo station many years ago, I set off with a small safari up the Tsavo river. Shortly after leaving Tsavo station I passed the lonely grave of a young French girl, all alone in that hard piece of Africa's treacherous " wait-a-bit " thorn bush. I read the inscription and wondered. It seemed so cold—one in a vast area.

Reaching the river, I followed up a game track, and within the first mile I spotted a brown object ahead of me. On stopping and taking my glasses I saw it was a lion, but what a spectacle ! Its skin was shrivelled up, and it was the most emaciated mangy specimen I have yet seen. It bunched itself together, wanted to charge, but had not the

E

life to do so. Its flesh was weak. I shot it, and saw where it had been trying to dig out snail shells from the side of the bank. There were marks of hyænas all round this place, where the animals evidently waited at night until finally his strength to defend himself would fail.

Now here was the type of lion which would not be averse to eating any kind of flesh and reduced to his final hunting stage by using his cunning, waylaying any unsuspecting animal which used that path. This lion had evidently been previously wounded, and it was a sense of satisfaction to know that I put him out of harm's way.

It is surprising to know the distances which lions will travel at night. I have seen their spoor in the sandy desert country where the next water was at least twenty miles away, and I am certain they will even travel up to thirty miles in one night. I remember seeing where a pride had actually fed on a swarm of locusts and they evidently became over-gorged, and in several places there were clusters of these insects vomited up which appeared to have been swallowed whole.

That the African lion has taken a big toll of sportsmen throughout Africa is evidenced by the sad eulogies seen in the different African churchyards—" Died from Lion Wounds." These words convey a great deal, and yet even today, with man armed with the most modern rifle, the chances with a really charging lion are pretty well even. You shoot at him—he will ever be prized as a trophy—and he goes into bush to await you. I have never seen a lion attempt to charge over sixty yards distance. He is cunning and brave, and waits until he is certain of getting his charge home. He or she stands—one or two lashes with that jerking, twisting upturned tail, and he comes. His feet do not appear to be touching the ground. He is bunched up and momentarily halts as he attempts to pull you with his outstretched claws to his open mouth. It is a terrifying experience, and the man who can stop one of these beasts coming as described can be relied upon taking the rough with the smooth—it is a good fifty-fifty chance. This is the respect I hold for the charging king of beasts when he does make that determined onslaught. The danger is in shooting too quickly, and it certainly takes a cool nerve to wait until he reaches a certain spot your brain and eye in conjunction have already selected. This is where the short arm would still give you a sporting chance should you fail to stop him with your rifle. Usually the parts he tries for are the thighs and arms.

His sense of smell is keen and will direct him to a kill up to half a mile distant. At the same time, he will be guided by the howls of hyænas or the bark of the jackal, and his keen eyes will even scan the horizon for vultures swooping down from the sky on to some carcase. He will kill if he is forced to, but actually prefers bait given. I am informed that this is entirely different from the wary tiger in India, and on account of the lion being easily enticed to bait he is much easier to secure. Antelope do not appear to be alarmed by the presence of lions, and I have actually watched them graze quite unconcerned within a few hundred yards of them. Zebra, wildebeest and eland, however, if they catch the smell of lions, will stampede and turn round and look in their direction, giving you often a valuable clue as to where the lions are lying up. Should you surprise one of these big cats asleep, he will invariably bolt and grunt in contempt as he does so. Having actually seen, without exaggeration, many thousands of them, I have never seen one charge back unmolested. Should you run foul of the lioness with cubs, there is always that danger, but often I have come across their lair, which was vacated evidently at my presence, and where there is a way to go she will take it.

This will show that lions in our game areas which are not disturbed will seldom if ever interfere with you and simply want to go their own free way. Still, man's sporting spirit wishes it otherwise and here is cunning pitted against wits.

I Trip Over a Lion

"SIMBA" is the Swahili word meaning "lion." Kenya boasts of a railway station of the same name, which lies about ninety miles south of Nairobi, the capital of Kenya Colony.

Many years ago this place was the Mecca for visiting sportsmen, and many good lions were obtained.   The railway is the dividing line between game reserve and shooting grounds, and there was always the big possibility of good-maned specimens finding their way over into the non-reserve. The country here is ideal for these big cats; the ground is sandy, plenty of cover, and well watered. Game is also plentiful, and there is no lack of food, always a big attraction.

Twelve years ago a party, including myself, wished to hunt here and selected a donga in which there were several reed-beds and likely places for holding lions.   They could kill game on the adjacent plains and return to lie up in the shade of the large trees overlooking this stream. The method taken was for the party to divide, one portion walking down the ravine on either side, while natives threw stones into the reed patches to scare any animals out.   It was late in the afternoon, and having hunted this ravine for a mile without success we were on the point of returning to camp. At the last stone pitched, there were several grunts and five lions bolted, breaking away on the opposite bank. Several shots were fired and the result was—one lion dead and a second wounded. The latter doubled back behind one of the porters and re-entered the donga we had driven. The man who fired at this lion was certain it was hit in the shoulder and could not live. As dusk was setting in, it was agreed we should leave it until the light was better and our hunt for this wounded animal would begin the following day.

Next morning our party was arranged and down we went to find the lion, expecting to come across it lying dead. Taking the beat down from some distance above which he entered, stones were pelted to drive him out, the party taking the same procedure as the previous evening. Within a few hundred yards there was an angry grunt, and I actually thought the lion was going to break in on my side of the stream. In the meantime there was a commotion on the opposite side as the lion broke out, charged up the embankment and spotted a porter who was carrying a luncheon basket on his head. This native ran, but in a second or so the lion was on him, knocking him down, and commenced mauling him. My friend on the same side as the boy rushed forward and shot the lion on top of the boy, but not before severe injuries were inflicted.

The danger and difficulty in this case lay in the fact that it was dangerous to shoot the lion lest the bullet would also kill the boy. As it was, I had my doubts as to a certain wound on the boy's arm, but then with the lion shaking the boy about and the eagerness to get in a shot, these things can happen. On examining this lion, it was found that the bullet from the rifle on the previous night had only lacerated the back hock, the sinews of which were licked like white cotton. Now the fact that this lion passed two other people on the way within a few yards—who stood fascinated by the terrible onrush—and tore past after the boy who had run, proved it never took its gaze from him the moment it charged from the reeds. This native was wonderful, and it was really surprising to see how he bore the pain of a severe mauling without even flinching. He was perfectly calm and did not utter a sound. He was attended to, placed in a blanket, and carried to a point on the Uganda Railway where the passenger train proceeding to Nairobi was stopped. He was conveyed to hospital, where his arm was amputated. This native recovered and today is tending his own herds of stock after his experiences in the grip of a savage lion.

Men who have been mauled tell me that the lion just shakes you as a dog does a rat. When you are still he watches you and would probably leave you, but one movement, and he will renew the attack ferociously. Blood poisoning usually sets in very quickly after being mauled on account of the filth that accumulates, chiefly on the claws. That preparation B.I.P. or a solution of permanganate of potash inserted into the wound is a fine precaution, but the main thing is to have it done as soon as possible.

My next lion hunt happened in an area where a solitary old male had killed several cattle, and the owner was anxious that I would assist him in destroying it. That afternoon I shot a zebra as bait and arranged a small hide at the bottom of a thorn tree and bushed it securely all round. About 8 p.m., the marauder came along and approached the kill from the back of my boma, but evidently he saw my movement on account of the opening on the top being reflected by the light of a quarter moon. I continued my all-night vigil, hearing the unmistakable breathing some yards behind, and always the alarmed gallop told me I was spotted. He left early in the morning. Hyænas kept coming all night long to feast on the kill, and I used all the pebbles I could find to throw at them. I then made a plan to alter this hide and move it towards some bush which would probably give the lion more confidence. The bait also would be more tempting for him. After lying another day under the African sun my hopes ran high for his returning the following night.

Meeting a friend, he expressed a desire to shoot this lion, to which I agreed. Everything arranged, we made ourselves really comfortable, placing a blanket on the earth, and in we went pyjama clad, a string or communication cord from the kill to our abode. The night being dark was in our favour, as this appeals to any wary animal. About 10 p.m. the lion appeared within a few yards of the kill and neither of us heard him approach; my friend used a ·450, fired a little quickly and hit him too far back and a little high in the shoulder. He spun round and growled, actually hitting the side of the boma, and then sprang forward again and disappeared.

Now it was obvious that unless we could recover him the hyænas would, and here was a good trophy going west. I heard him breathing some distance in front of the boma, and my friend flashing a torch actually saw him lying down. There was no sound or movement, and all round were the eyes of several hyænas watching and waiting to devour him. There was nothing else for it—I would push my thorn door outwards, and grabbing my pants and hastily pulling them on in the dark I went out in the direction of the lion. He was only fifty yards away, but looking in the dark with the torch he appeared double this distance. Going very cautiously, suddenly my friend's torch ceased to function. I tripped over the top of this lion in the darkness. He made a move and I fled back to that boma as fast as my legs would go, discovering as I raced that I was hampered in my stride, as I had my trousers on back to front. I only did fifty yards, but my readers may not be surprised to know that I was perspiring freely. That I made a mistake there was not the slightest doubt, but then in darkness everything appears so different and misleading. We left that lion until daybreak and found him unspoilt. He was an old beast and his head and neck were scarred with claw and tooth, evidently caused by fighting with others.

A few days later I was breakfasting when a herd of zebra came galloping past the back of our camp.

Seeing an object coming behind I was surprised to spot a fine tawny-maned lion following them. Telling my friend there was a lion coming, he evidently took it as a joke and was dubious. While waiting, this lion spotted our camp and doubled back to a small ravine, the banks of which were deep, and in places the bush was sparse where you could easily see across to the opposite side. My friend now, seeing I was in earnest, picked up his rifle and we cut over some few hundred yards in front to intercept him. We were in splendid time and here was a wonderful sight, this lion wandering down the ravine on our side and towards us. He kept stopping and looking back to see if we were following, little suspecting that the S-shaped bend of the donga had betrayed him. My friend, now keen to get a choice specimen, put up his gun and pulled the trigger. There was no report—a click. He had failed to put a cartridge in the chamber from the magazine, instead of loading.

Quickly he commenced to curse himself for the omission, and in the meantime the lion heard and trotted off, disappearing down the incline for a thick patch of bush. Telling him to fire, he did, and the lion spun round, growling savagely, and made for the thick bush. Coming up to the place where he entered, I found a piece of splintered bone from the hind leg, and from the tracks in the mud the bone was fractured and he was travelling on three sound legs and a hind stump. Now a lion even in this state can travel or charge for a short distance as quickly as if he had four sound legs, and there was every possibility here of a dangerous hunt. We decided to follow, and the bush was anything but inviting on account of briars and sisal, the tips of the latter being hard, sharp and painful should you come in contact with them. Ahead you could see where he crashed through at no mean speed.

Now this patch did not cover more than one hundred yards and it was obvious he would never leave it, but would probably push forward and make a fight within sight of the other end. Going carefully, ever cautious, you wonder if he is waiting, watching for you behind that bush in front. You are keyed up—your rifle ready to be thrown up at a fraction of a second to stop the mad rush as he comes. The silence in bush like that is a bit eerie; you do not hear even the chirp of a bird— a dik-dik or small antelope scutters past you, the noise in the undergrowth scaring the life out of you as he breaks. There is more blood now and he is walking slowly, but still the mark of the fractured bone taking its stride. In the distance you can see light through the bush ahead of you—you will soon know the worst or the best. Coming within fifty yards of the edge of the bush, you spot a tiny black spot moving. It is the back of his ear tips; he is sitting down, and his head is not looking in your direction. You whisper to your friend that you see him and he is also anxious to get a glimpse. The lion hears, is up in a frenzy, and comes growling at you with ears flattened back to his head and tail straight up. He is hampered in breaking through some twining briars and receives two shots, falling where he was hit.   He is a splendid lion and it is a pity the thorns he charged through robbed him of portions of his fine mane.

I have seen many lions shot through the forearm, breaking the bone, yet they will charge through, and it is really surprising the distance and speed they can come, even with only three sound legs. Their valour and courage when wounded and in cover can never be disputed.

A Dutch hunter in Tanganyika Territory a few years ago, when hunting near Ngorongoro Crater, had the unique experience of seeing two maned lions standing up in combat.   The noise was deafening, and he fired at the shoulder of one, using a ·350 Rigby Magnum rifle, with solid bullet, and imagine his surprise to see them fall to the shot, the bullet traversing both animals.

Man-Eating Lions

IN several parts of Africa (I will include Portuguese East) man-eating lions have caused panic and consternation amongst the local natives and others, rewards being offered for their destruction. A friend of mine was hunting down there some years ago and arrived at a certain camp where several natives had been taken. Making his camp in the late evening, his native cook-boy, hearing the reports from other natives, begged that he might sleep on the floor, where he would be safe beside his master's rifle. My friend after supper put down his mosquito net and turned in to sleep with a rifle close beside him, while the cook-boy curled up on the floor. The front curtain of the tent was left partly open, and imagine my friend's surprise when he woke up in the morning to find his cook missing, and his blanket lying torn outside the tent door. Now it seems incredible to understand or believe that. The boy was picked up from the floor inside the tent and yet Mr. —— never heard a sound.

I have been informed by natives who live in those parts that the look of a mosquito net—frail as it is—is a deterrent against lions, and I have not heard an instance where anyone has even been molested while under a mosquito net.

77

It seems ridiculous. The remains of this cook
boy were found next day nearly 200 yards away,
a lioness, mangy and thin, being the culprit.
She was found to be suffering from an old gunshot
wound. Many of the natives own muzzle-loading
rifles, shooting slugs and even pebbles, and it is
not surprising why so many animals get away
wounded, and are in consequence a danger and
a menace to all in the vicinity.

I had occasion to follow two lions in fairly open
country, and vultures hovering in the vicinity
meant these lions had a kill near by. Seeing some
of these birds perched on a tree, I went cautiously
forward and there in a clump of bush, lying on
their sides, were two large maneless lions. I could
see the side of one of them moving up and down as
he breathed, and I fired, hitting him behind the
shoulder. At the report the other one, which was
facing my way, sprang out of that bush and leapt
right over the top of my head, knocking off my
terai hat. I had not time to shoot, but just stood
amazed. Evidently the blast of the rifle gave him
a terrible awakening, and in his fear he sprang out
to escape, and not to charge me. The first one
was quite dead, but I never managed to come up
with the second.

Twelve years ago, in the tsetse fly area, eight
fine lions were bagged in a night by an intrepid
Scots sportswoman. While the hunt lasted, the
atmosphere resounded with growls and thrills.
At this time in Eastern Africa there was no limit
to the number of lions allowed on a licence, and

our camp was pitched amongst some large trees on the banks of a small rocky stream. It was our intention to trek down this water-course and move to the west to pass the fly belt, but shooting a buffalo on the way delayed us, and we had no recourse but to spend the night there. The natives attached to our safari brought loads of meat back to the camp, and were soon busy cutting it up in strips and partly cooking it over their camp fires. Shortly after dusk, a regular chorus of lions grunting was heard close to our camp. It was then that the natives all appeared to have contracted colds, as they commenced coughing, with the idea that the noise would scare the lions off. From the noise created, it was evident the troop was a large one and had several old males. The really old fellows had wonderful lung power, and we arranged to try for them the next morning. The smell of the meat attracted them and they kept grunting continuously throughout the night. After you have been in the African bush for many years, you find yourself getting accustomed to these animals' roars and can fall asleep listening to them. There is something grand about the wildness of it.

Next morning we heard them at 5 a.m., but from the sound it was evident they were heading for the hills three miles off. It was obvious they had not fed on account of their hanging round the camp for meat, and should we fail to come up with them in the day, we would wait for them next night. What a night was in store for us ! Hunting during the day, we circled the lower slopes of that hill, and actually saw signs where they had lain and even fed, but failed to connect with them. A herd of buffalo were seen in this area, but we refrained from shooting lest the lions heard the shots and decamped. That afternoon, west of the camp, we shot a zebra and wildebeest, which were coming down to drink at the stream where our tents were pitched, and with the aid of boys we cut them in sections on account of their weight and dragged them to a suitable place where the lions had lain the night before. The bush was low and leafless, and at length a suitable site was selected where our bait was pegged down and a hide in the ground was made of thorn bushes. Inside the space was roughly six by six feet, and here we would wait our feline guests.

At dusk we moved into our hide, which was not more than 200 yards from the camp, and while there the natives laughing in camp could be distinctly heard. Soon two jackals appeared, and trotting round, sat down quite close to the kill. Now jackals always give lions confidence, and our plan was, let them eat, they had plenty of meat to feed on. When darkness set in, a hyæna slunk up, twisting his tail in their peculiar fashion. When I tapped the bush he scuttled off, and at last getting brave, or used to the sound, he commenced to feed, usually grabbing a piece of the entrails and running off with it, only to return for more when finished.

I was surprised we had not heard the lions up to this time, as the previous night they had been on the scene so much earlier on. Lions are prone to this inquisitiveness. On your first night they usually want to find out who's who, and after this their curiosity dies off. The hyæna, coming back, commenced to feed, and within a few minutes looked behind and galloped off right past the side of our hide. Now here was the certain sign of lions coming, otherwise he would not have gone. The lions, seeing the hyæna on the meat, rushed forward, and in the next few minutes there was a large pride in front of us, growling savagely, while those underneath were whining, and the whole place seemed a moving, swaying mass. I was trying to point out the largest to the lassie beside me, and don't think she even heard; her eyes were glued on that struggling, growling, hungry mob. She fired, and I saw the largest male lunge forward, cannoning into another as he fell. Now the growling and snarling commenced proper and the voices of our boys in camp stopped automatically. With the use of a torch I could see the big lion; his mane was poor. He was lying quite dead. Then I heard the pad or silent tread of something beside our hide. Within a few minutes on came another lion. I watched him sniff at the dead one, and then looking round he commenced feeding. When this happened, the others seemed to come from nowhere, they were all back on to that carcase and eating ravenously. I switched a torch on the centre of them. They all stopped eating and stared intently in our direction. At this moment the rifle spat again and another male reared and spun round and round, while another lion attacked him savagely.

F

The aggressor now received a bullet in the base of the neck, and there were three lions, all males and big ones, practically lying against each other.

From this time onwards there was quite a lull, during which time the remainder went wandering round the camp and began half grunting and roaring in unison. Now this scared the lives out of the boys in camp, and many of them climbed up the trees close by, where they remained until morning. Shortly after midnight the remainder of this pride of lions (there were ten altogether, which we had reduced, to seven) returned to the kill and commenced feeding. They came on silently and stood for several minutes looking and listening as if to find out where their enemies were hidden. They did not have long to wait, as Mrs. —— took a right and left at two standing in the centre of the group, and two more of those big cats bit the dust. Now here were five lions, with so many shots and all killed on the spot. Admitted they were killed at close range, but I have seen many lions missed through over-excitement at the same distance.

I can recollect the sportsman who had done a lot of shooting, and in using his double rifle, after firing his first shot, complained of the left barrel not going off, and I discovered he was trying to pull his first trigger twice. This, I would add, was a double trigger gun. Then again, I have seen another shooter pulling the trigger of his magazine rifle twice, forgetting to work the bolt action to reload. Still, excitement can account for many different things.

I trust my readers will excuse me for leaving my narrative to mention these side issues.

About 3 a.m. the remaining five lions returned, and we let them stay beside the kill for at least half an hour to give them confidence. During that time they had a false alarm and galloped off. They stood some distance away before venturing forward again. My lady now placed herself in position to take the next largest specimen, and no sooner did the Queen of Beasts walk past than her rifle boomed, and there was a tremendous roar. The lioness was hit too far back and she made one rush in our direction and actually tried to get into our hide. Her head was underneath our flimsy structure and she was doing her best to get through. But for two sticks in the ground on to which the brushwood was tied, she must surely have done so. This lioness, a very big one, was actually shot in our hide, at least the head was. I am not prepared to say that this was an actual attempt to charge us, as it may have been by fear at the sight of the other dead lions beside her. Be it so, even if she had managed to get through, imbued by fear, it might have been awkward. I was—in fact, we both were—pleased when the signs of dawn appeared in the east. Time seems so delayed when you are waiting for the hours to pass, especially with living and dead lions around you.

At 5.45 a.m. I heard the other lions grunting quite near us beyond some scrubby bush on our left. We walked slowly through, and there in an open patch were four of them waiting for the remainder of their troop to return. We were within fifty yards of them and yet they had not detected our presence. Selecting the biggest, Mrs. —— fired, hitting him in the base of the ear, and he simply dropped instanter. The remaining three stood up and slunk away—a mob without a leader. Another one was shot, which, however, necessitated three bullets, and the two remaining galloped off in the direction of the hills.

When we returned to camp our natives had wonderful tales to tell of the night before and how the lions had taken possession of the camp, etc., but then this is typical of the natives' stretch of imagination. Wanderobo natives, these nomads who had large herds of sheep in this vicinity, came next day and thanked us for having wiped out this mob of lions, which had in the past taken considerable toll from their stock.

The largest lion, which was the first shot from this troop, is mentioned in Rowland Ward's " Records of Big Game," ninth edition, and it measured 10 feet 1 inch. Skinning these eight lions occupied the most of the next day, but this was the largest bag of lions I have seen accounted for on a single night.

So here ends another night of watching and waiting for lions.

Now I wish to impress on the reader that when you go out after lions, you do not get them always charging. I have had and seen lions run with their tails pressed down, and the very essence of fright and flight. But these anecdotes and incidents

I relate have happened over a quarter of a century
and amongst a large number of lions. Even in
this part about which I write, there are still many
lions today. The district is fairly accessible and
as yet uninhabited. Should any of my readers
camp by that same stream and hunt in the same
area, you will find your lions, and, as then, some of
them fierce and many not so. The area I refer
to is twenty miles due south of Bordomat in the
Southern Masai Reserve in Kenya Colony.

Fifteen miles further west of this camp, and on the
same stream, where the banks are much steeper,
I accompanied a sporting Colonel of the British
Army. We hunted lions for several days and
always seemed to be just a few hours late. We
found where they had been and moved. During
one late afternoon we found a topi (an antelope)
kill near a small dry watercourse, and it looked as
if lions had recently left. Following the spoor,
which continued in wide circles, we eventually
lost it, and in returning through some dense bush
discovered a magnificent black mane standing over
his own kill, a picture of defiance and a magnificent
sight. My friend fired at a range of twenty yards
and he dropped dead. Afterwards it took us some
time to find the wound which caused his death,
the bullet having entered his mouth, between the
incisors, without making a mark. My friend had
a look of alarm when I informed him the lion had
died from fright ! This was a beautiful lion, with
that dark sheen over the whole skin and flanks
right down to the point of his tail. We put some

branches over the lion and proceeded to the camp
to get some porters to bring it in. When we returned, a hyæna was standing over the dead lion,
and the livid Colonel gave vent to his vocabulary.
I take off my hat to that Colonel—his oaths at
that hyæna and its ancestors surpassed my imagination. He swore for several minutes, never repeating
himself. I envied him his velvety flow.

Near this camp a large elephant was seen mean-
dering amongst some sparse bush. My friend
hurried back to camp, returning with his Holland
·465 rifle. We proceeded in the direction the
elephant was feeding and shot him. He was a
sitter and gave no trouble whatsoever. Now here
was an idea. Lions seldom get a chance of elephant
meat, because as a general rule elephants are not
found in the best lion areas. Yet here was a huge
bull, at least six tons of meat, in their very midst.
This elephant carried tusks of 74 and 76 lb. respectively, a good weight in this particular part. I
have often wondered why elephants in some localities carry heavier ivory than in others. I have
never heard anyone refer to it. Yet, the weight in
ivory on the general average must be attributed to
some particular cause, maybe on account of the
feeding, possibly lime, or some other stimulant
which promotes the growth, from salt licks they
partake of so freely. Some of these licks are of a
distinct clay composition, and I have often seen
broken points of tusks lying under where they dig
into the hardened banks. It would be interesting
to analyse these soils and learn what actual proper-

ties they contain. Let us hope that someone more authoritative will furnish facts which may probably throw some light on these excessive weights.

Even the insect life—butterflies in particular—are most partial to salt brackish water. In the Northern Congo I have seen myriads of them feeding and fluttering on these alkaline waters, and though in other places they are troublesome to capture, yet on these salt marshes they lose their entire sense of wariness. I am convinced that in many veins natural history is still in its infancy, but I am only passing my opinion. Possibly it may be poor on subjects of which I know little, but I trust that someone more competent will take up the matter.

Returning to our elephant lying cold in the midst of Kenya's best lion country, I found our team of oxen had covered a large circuit and met us at our present camp. The driver in charge of these oxen was a South African native, and his methods in handling a team of thirty-two animals were second to none. He never abused his team, yet always managed to get the most out of them. Each animal had his name and knew it, and each one pulled his share. The crack of that long giraffe-skin thonged whip, echoed over those plains. He was certainly the best handler of oxen transport I have ever seen in my varied travels. His weakness was gin, and his strength handling oxen. Yet with all his failings, he was a gentleman of the African veldt.

Visiting the elephant carcase next morning showed the spoor of countless hyænas, and a few lions. Parts of the trunk had been chewed and eaten as well as round the edges of the soles. The elephant had now become blown and expanded to alarming proportions on account of the formation of stomach gases. We set to building a hide with branches and thorns within five yards of it, and when completed the Colonel thought we had made a mistake in not having it even nearer. The only way to alter this was to get our team of oxen, and with the aid of a heavy trek chain have the carcase pulled closer. Getting the oxen hitched on was only a matter of minutes, but it was soon found to be unworkable. The oxen strained and pulled, but they could not move that mountain of blown-up flesh. Fastening the chain round the hind legs was next attempted, and this ended in making matters worse—the legs slewed round and nearly touched our boma.

The general survey, as it now appeared, was similar to a small enclosure, the back of the elephant carcase facing to the east and our boma to the west, and the only access for the animals was past the elephant's hind feet. A pole with a small pan attached to hold flare powder was fixed, and in daylight it looked quite practicable. Entering the boma that evening all expectant, we did not have long to wait until darkness set in, when the weird dismal howls of the hyænas commenced. Now the smell of this rotting mass must have wafted many miles over those plains, and as the African winds continually change, the carnivorous creatures evidently picked up the strong scent from many directions.

Lion attracted by the latter, and the howling mob of Africa's scavengers, were heard grunting in the distance all heading on to our bait. It was thrilling, to say the least, sitting there and listening to all the different sounds emitted by the denizens of the bush. On they came, and the teeth and claws of the lions could easily be discerned rasping at the skin on the back of the elephant. The skin of the carcase was absolutely taut, and the noise reminded us of scratching on a drum. There must have been twenty lions round the back of this carcase, but they appeared shy and would not enter in front. It looked too much like a trap for their liking. I peered out in the early morning, and there was a huge lioness standing on top of the blown-up side of the elephant, and looking straight into our hide. I moved—she saw me— and with one deep guttural grunt sprang back on to the ground at the back of the carcase. After this happened, several males commenced roaring, evidently aware of danger, their deep bass awe-inspiring notes making the very ground vibrate. I am sure many of my readers would have been overjoyed and thrilled to have had the opportunity of sitting there and listening to the deep sighs and magic notes emitted by these monarchs of the veldt. I do not know any other animal's voice to compare. The elephant's piercing high-pitched scream is decidedly blood-curdling, but the sound of several big lions, giving vent to their loudest, is beyond any comparison.

The night so far had been unsuccessful, we had

taken no pictures, and it was evident we must make a larger opening to ensure success. Next morning, after daybreak, several lions could be seen slinking off, which were evidently loth to leave on account of the large number of vultures all sitting and hovering near the kill.

Placing a blanket on a pole beside the kill, to scare off the vultures, we returned to camp, had breakfast, and rearranged our boma. The whole carcase was now a mass of blow-flies, and the stench when the wind bore it towards us was beyond description. In fact, it was perfectly clear that it would be well-nigh impossible to abide by that rotting mass after tonight. Gases whistled and sizzled from the carcase, and we moved our abode to a distance of ten yards off, which, as we found out that night, was yet too near, and returned to our carcase at 6 p.m. with handkerchiefs employed as gas masks. The vultures, which had been waiting patiently all day, actually came down *en masse* and commenced to tear an opening through the hide. That the flanks were now beginning to get softer was evinced by the manner in which these vultures commenced tearing with their powerful beaks.

While there was still light, a lioness rushed up and scattered that huge mob of carrion-eaters, and sat down in full possession. Here was a good start, and she sat there just surveying the animal, her head following any bird which passed overhead. Within the next hour, or even less, you could distinguish the low, jerky, short grunts of lions coming from three different directions. On they came, and the temerity of the previous night had entirely disappeared. We watched these lions, different troupes, intermingle. There were many large lions, and at one time I counted twenty feeding amongst the bunch. I spotted a lioness with three soft woolly-clad cubs. I do not think they were more than four months old, and yet they were probably being initiated into their first elephant meal.

We had evidence of a most interesting night before us, which was, however, marred by another cause, actually accentuated by the lions themselves. While the hungry mass was tearing, ripping, intermingled with short grunts and snarling, there was a rushing sound, similar to steam escaping from a siren, and the stomach of the elephant literally blew up. I cannot find words to describe the unimaginable stench. At the explosion we were heavily sprayed, and for the time being the lions actually cleared *en masse*, and we would have done likewise had it been possible. But to sit there in that choking atmosphere, inhaling Africa's worst poison gas, is one of my worst experiences, which I will ever remember. The position became quite untenable, not on account of the lions, but from the poisoned air, and when you get too much of the latter you forget the former. Making up our minds quickly, we fired several shots in the air and you could hear the lions gallop at the reports. We pushed back our thorns from the boma, which were used as the door, cleared out into the night and left the place, keeping close together as we walked. Several forms slunk or raced past us, but we were not interfered with and reached camp, once more breathing the pure air of Africa.

I have not taken the trouble to sit by another dead elephant, and if my readers are ever tempted to try this, be sure you guard against the fumes of a similar explosion.

It may seem strange to the average reader to know that at a mean estimate 75 per cent. of the European population in Africa have seldom seen a wild lion, as the lions which grunt in darkness near civilisation are seldom seen, and those which roam on the fringes of our vast plains are so far away that they cannot be seen without taking an organised expedition.

That Tanganyika Territory holds the most lions in the world today in any one territory there is no disputing. In the best game centres far from the pale of mankind, their only enemy, lions, never live in thick cover unless forced to, but prefer to lie up for the day near the fringe of bush or by the banks of ravines, where they have a fair view of the surrounding area.

Two sportsmen who had never seen an uncaged lion were keen on trying their luck and set off to the Simba district, some 230 miles by rail from Mombasa, with a view to shooting some. At this time there were grass fires all over the district, which was in their favour, as the country having a blackened appearance, game are easily discernible.

In their first day's stroll to look for Africa's biggest cats, they travelled far and saw none. On the return towards camp, some animals were seen which they took to be hartebeest, and the two shooters commenced their stalk over the recently burned ground, making themselves much the same colour. Their stalk was a long and good one. On getting closer, binoculars were brought into play. No. 1 looked anxious and said, " They are lions." No. 2 had a look and with alarm said, " By Gad, you're right," and suffering from the effects of cold feet, they returned to camp.

A Lion's Breath

IT was within twenty miles of this place that I had a close shave with a large maneless lion, and will ask my readers to read and travel with me on this hunt.

I strolled down the side of a stream with a shot-gun to get some partridge or spur-fowl for the pot, and on a stretch of volcanic dusty ground I noticed dust being raised by flocks of guinea-fowl which were scratching in the soft earth for grit or food. Approaching them, taking all the cover I could, as their running powers are extraordinary if they notice you, I nearly walked on two large lions which were evidently asleep. I don't know who was scared most—I doubt if anyone could have retreated quicker than I did. In fact, we were both travelling in opposite directions, my safety distance. I did not want to shoot at birds, as the sound would disturb the lions, and secondly, I did not feel too happy with only a 12-bore gun in my hands.

On the following morning I revisited this place, taking a rifle with me, while my native carried a shot-gun. In scouting round, we came across the remains of a wildebeest, which the two lions had fed on the previous day. Following up a sand river, we came on a small spring, and it was clear to us that these two lions had drunk there early that morning. The going was excellent, and my boy in scanning from a tree noticed the two lions of the day before. They were just over a ridge and evidently in the habit of killing game which came down to drink at this spring. There was practically no wind, and we commenced crawling along on our stomachs, I pushing the rifle in front of me and getting up to it again. It was slow work, and within an hour we were within shot of them. From where we lay I could see the lions distinctly, and saw that the largest lion was of a maneless type, having only one thick ridge down the top of his neck, while the other—the smaller—lion had a nice mane, mostly tawny, but quite dark on his chest and shoulders. Selecting the latter, I fired, hitting him on the point of the shoulder. He reared to the shot and I promptly gave him a second bullet while on his hind legs. The large maneless beast galloped for the donga and I made a poor exhibition as he crossed at right angles, missing twice, both my bullets going over him.

Following up, I followed his tracks for some time, but eventually lost them in the thick scrub adjoining the sand river. Late that afternoon I shot a zebra as a bait for the lion, knowing he would not leave the vicinity until next day, and I brushed it over with thorn to keep it from the keen eyes of the ever-hovering vultures. That night, this lion returned, and kept up an incessant series of short roars and gruntings. He seemed to travel in wide circles, ever calling for the one I had killed that day. This prowling round continued until 5 a.m., and as it was nearing daybreak the sound of his last grunt gave me a sense of direction, in which line I followed as soon as it was light enough to see the foresight of my rifle.

Passing the dead zebra, which I had placed for bait, I found it untouched. There was the lion's spoor beside it and yet he had not attempted to eat. Scaling an ant-hill beyond, we sat there waiting, knowing that as soon as the sun appeared he might give another grunt. This would direct me. I was not disappointed. We heard the gruff, low, husky grunt on the other side of the river towards a place where there was a patch of unburnt grass. I cut across to the sand river and followed upstream towards the place where I last heard him and peered over the top. His eyes were quicker than mine and he streaked his fastest towards a thick green patch of low bush. I fired, knowing that my chance was not a good one on account of the long dry grass, and at the shot he gave a savage grunt and, lashing his tail, disappeared in the thicket. The bush he entered was practically on top of the bank of this sand river, and it was unlikely he would attempt to slip down the off side. Several francolin which had evidently been roosting there flew out in alarm.

And now to get the lion out. Approaching with caution, we came nearer and nearer the bush in which he lay, evidently watching us, but he did not utter a sound. When within fifteen yards I stopped, determined to go no closer, and here I made a mistake. I took my eyes off the bush to pick up a piece of transparent quartz on the ground, and was in the act of throwing it into the thicket, when he sprang at me with a terrible roar. He looked colossal in mid-air. I do not remember even aiming, I am certain I just fired my heavy rifle as if it had been a scatter gun. I actually felt his hot clammy breath in my face as he fell from my height in front of me. As he lay on the ground, his head between his massive forearms, showing the hole between the eyes caused by bullet and powder at practically muzzle range, I was strangely fascinated as I watched the smoke ooze out in curls from that fatal wound. Here lay the bravest and most courageous animal the veldt could offer, and so aptly described as the king of beasts.

This lion measured 10 feet long before skinning, and was in perfect condition, while the fine maned specimen shot the previous day was 9 feet 4 inches.

From my personal experience, I say that the speed of the charging lion is exceptional, the spring well-timed and only steady and accurate shooting can save you. Natives who have been mauled and bore tooth marks to substantiate their experience have informed me that they were in each case attacked and lacerated by his enormous claws. When they lay still, feigning death, the lion would leave them and sit a few yards distant and watch as a cat would a mouse, and if no movement within five minutes he would leave the scene, but if any part was moved the lion would return to the attack and then use both teeth and claws and shake the victim as a dog does a rat.

G

The claws of the lion and leopard are always more or less poisoned with particles of decomposed meat and blood, and it is absolutely essential that any wounds sustained should be washed clean and disinfected, and anti-gangrene preparation inserted immediately. Several persons so mauled have lost heart and hope from even minor scratches, maybe on account of shock to the system, and invariably with fatal results.

CHAPTER NINE

Filming the Blankety-Blank

FROM the serious to the humorous came about one day on the Loita Plains in the Southern Masai Reserve in Kenya.

I accompanied a film fan, keen on getting a really good lion picture. The most likely place suitable for this was an isolated rocky kopje standing high in these vast windy plains. For several days I shot zebra in the vicinity, knowing full well that lions would be attracted and would seek refuge amongst the rocks during the daytime. On the fourth day I was satisfied the lions were there. Now was my friend's opportunity and off we went to the hill, taking twenty natives with us, all armed with gasoline cans, cooking pots, in fact all I could muster which would create a terrible din. The star rigged up his cine on a stout tripod, and the whole affair was beautifully camouflaged with branches to make it as inconspicuous as possible. I wanted to stay beside him, but the difficulty was, unless the beaters had someone to direct them, this drive would most probably end in failure. To overcome this, two trained gun-bearers were left beside the operator, while I accompanied the porters to encircle the kopje. A shot fired would be the signal when the drive actually commenced.

On the way round I spotted several lionesses

which slunk up amongst the rocks on the summit. This was indeed promising, and there would be no doubt as to close-up pictures being taken. It took some time getting my twenty porters in position, having several on the flanks about twenty yards forward from the centre line, which I thought would assist in preventing any lions breaking cover from the sides. When ready, I fired a shot-gun to give the alarm, and the drive commenced. The going on top I found very rough indeed, on account of the immense boulders, which were more like miniature caves. A boy yelled out, " Simbas " (lions), and I saw a pride of eight sneaking and walking slowly forward along the top of the ridge and going in the required direction. Now when lions' tails are heading from them, these boys are brave and yell the more.

About half-way the stench of lions and decayed meat was indeed strong, and a lioness with cubs came out grunting in our direction, and here my porters went in headlong flight, going back in the direction from which we had come. This big cat only made one rush, and I think her idea was to intimidate, and she went back again, in the same low crouching manner as the others had gone. Now these boys with their bare feet and legs went over that rough and sharp boulder ground with the same ease as if it were turf, and it was with difficulty I managed to get them all back into line again. I fired two more shots from my gun to give them confidence and the drive recommenced. I noticed that there were lions, lionesses, cubs, spotted and striped hyænas, all living together under the adjacent rocks, and when the drive was finished, which occupied only one hour, we had actually put up sixteen lions of all kinds and more than double that number of hyænas from that kopje. Only two lions broke cover from the north side of the hill, the remainder all sneaking past the cine, looking behind to see how close the beaters were following.

Now here we should have secured some of the best lion pictures taken on foot—and the disappointment ! My friend, who would allow no one to go near that apparatus lest a mistake should be made, had forgotten to remove the lens cap from the cine, and hereby spoiled another good picture. The drive had been most successful and the lions obliging. They only growled and put on speed when they realised they had passed within a few feet of the operator and gun bearers.

As I write this, there are still lions on that same kopje, and I trust, should you ever contemplate a similar drive, you will leave the lens cap at home.

There is a large salt marsh within fifteen miles of this plain which many years ago was the home of numerous lions and hyænas. This marsh used to be a regular halting-place for the ox-transport riders, before the automobile put in its appearance. On account of much bush surrounding the whole swamp, lions were seldom seen in the day-time, confining themselves to marauding at night.

Camping there one afternoon, I met two sportsmen who had recently arrived in the country, and their ambition was to shoot lions. I have noticed that lions always appeal most to the visitor. There is something majestic about the black-maned lion. He is a splendid, noble creature. They had evidently picked up information as to how to proceed and already had shot a zebra for bait which they would sit over that night. Examining their blind, I informed them it was quite unsafe, as it was simply built of a few thin saplings, offering no protection whatever. Taking my advice, they added to it, and said that they would wait that night in the dark and try their skill. About midnight their shooting commenced, and during the night and early hours at least a dozen shots were fired. From the camp, which was only 300 yards away, I heard hyænas howling their weird and dismal yells, but not the grunt of a lion. I wondered what they were shooting at.

Next morning one of the two sportsmen came over to my tent, terribly elated and excited. He was certain they had shot seven lions ! There was a slight, though remote, possibility that they had done so, as had there been this number of lions we must have heard them grunt or growl from the camp. Taking my boys, we visited the hide, and to his surprise and disgust, his trophies without exception were foul and hideous-looking spotted hyænas. These animals can emit peculiar bass grunts and noises which are very apt to mislead the newcomer.

During the next three days, however, these

sportsmen—I will now call them my friends—were successful in shooting three fine maned lions, which made up for their first hyæna-lion shoot.

Amongst the natives of Africa, the fat of the lion is eagerly sought for and highly prized as a certain remedy for rheumatism. Whether this is so or not I do not wish to pronounce an opinion, as it may only be based on the fact that the substance is taken from the strength of this powerful and courageous animal.

LOST IN THE AFRICAN BUSH

When lion hunting three years ago in the Taveta and Maktau areas, which lie south-east of Kilimanjaro, that magnificent snow-capped mountain 19,000 feet high, the highest in Africa, towering in all its glory over those vast and arid plains below —yea, a veritable sentinel of the African bush— we, a party of four, left in the early morning to hunt, going south into some little-known country, leaving one member in camp. On our return in the late evening, one of the personal boys came and reported that the European had left shortly after our departure that morning and had not returned. On visiting his tent, his terai hat was lying there, and I could not understand what had happened to him. I would mention that it was from this same camp that a well-known big-game hunter of many years' experience was mauled by a lion, and died shortly after being admitted into the Mombasa hospital from the effects. I was sorry for this hunter. He lost heart after being mauled, and his

words were, " I am done for," and he did not seem
to resist. Yet he was a strong man. Such is the
fight between man and beast.

Darkness came on—we have little twilight, if
any, in Eastern Africa. Henry had not returned.
Could he have run foul of a rhino or lion ? They
were both well represented here. I fired my rifle
to the north and south. I listened—no report.
This was distressing, and yet it was quite useless
to attempt to do anything in the darkness. The
African bush at night is an inhospitable place.
After supper I wandered down past the camp
and stopped near that graveyard, full of South
Africa's best and bravest sons, who died in action
in the last Great War, fighting in this vicinity. It
is certainly a fitting place for men far removed from
civilization, and yet cared for in the veldt. Here
are still the remains of the trenches in which they
fought, also many relics of other impedimenta of
war, slowly but surely rusting and crumbling under
the elements of the weather and the fierce tropical
sun.

AN EPITAPH

South Africa

By Afric's snow-capped peak o'ershadowed
    'Neath the sunlit veldt,
      Taveta and Maktau,
   Your gallant sons
      You to the nation gave
      Lie sleeping,
  Revered, loved and honoured,
    In Kenya's keeping.

Throughout the night we did not sleep, and a lamp was hoisted on a pole to direct Henry—I admit, a feeble effort. Next morning I collected two of my best trackers. These were Walungulu natives, who excel in tracking elephants, and they took up Henry's spoor from the time he had left camp, like blood-hounds. This was the first time I had followed a two-legged spoor, and it was interesting to watch these bush hounds. They trailed him to a rocky hill; here we found two empty cartridge shells and some feathers. Our next effort was to dodge two rhinoceros, which puffed and let off steam as if to challenge our authority. Letting them pass, we trailed on, and now the spoor began to take us in circles—a sure and certain indication of the depressing word " Lost." He had realised his mistake, but a little late. The African bush is so much alike and it is extraordinarily simple to lose your bearings, and here was Henry trying to find his way back. The earth is hard and sandy, and leaves little impression unless to the cultivated eye. How these boys worked—they seldom spoke, only pointed with a small twig at some slight abrasion on the hard stony surface. The marks were now towards Ngulia mountains, at least twenty miles north, and the fact that Henry was under the hot tropical sun without a hat, food, water or help was an unenviable predicament.

Some few miles further on we found two guinea-fowl and his gun beside a thorn tree. Here was a sure sign—a man, alone in Africa, beaten. That he had discarded his gun was indeed serious. Those

Walungulu natives never left his track.   They could even tell when he stopped, and their bush-craft seemed superhuman.   It was now getting on to midday when they found him, having spoored him in circles at least twenty miles.

Poor Henry—his expression when he saw them ! but he was too done in to take much notice, and this in less than two days.   But two days on the Equator under that piercing sun can be equivalent to much more under other climes.   With water and food he soon recovered from his ordeal, and in his own words: " I suffered hell."   Lions had grunted near him and rhinos puffed, but he was too much otherwise concerned to take any notice of them. We returned to camp late that night, and apart from severe headaches due to the effects of the sun, Henry soon recovered.   It appeared that he heard guinea-fowl calling near the camp and followed them, and in his excitement he was actually lost in the first mile of leaving camp.   But for my Walungulu guides, there would probably have been one more name inscribed on Africa's casualty list.

One cannot but look back on our ancestors.   I will claim relationship in spirit with those wonderful African hunters who in times past used muzzle-loading guns, against our present-day breech-loading self-ejecting pieces of efficiency.   When you think of their two bare shots—and nothing else between them and a dangerous antagonist without reloading, one cannot but admire those premier sportsmen of their times. Names, great names, like Baker and Selous, whose doings can never die. Conditions and times have entirely changed since their great days, and I often wonder in our present-day hurried walk of life if the sporting spirit of those days, the days of our grandfathers, was not of a higher standard than it is to-day.

Africa still holds her attractions, her spell, and her yet untrodden ways, for anyone so inclined to visit the by-ways far removed from the intrusion of mankind.

A GRIEF-STRICKEN WIDOW

I will describe it. A party of sportsmen, including the wife of the head of the expedition, visited Africa's shores, the object in view being to hunt in Eastern and Central Africa. Most of the equipment and stores were shipped from the States, and on the whole it was practically an entirely American equipped expedition. The main object of this safari was scientific, and would also include a certain amount of hunting.

Proceeding to Tanganyika Territory for a month prior to proceeding to French Equatorial Africa, it was suggested to try and obtain a group of lions, and on their arrival in camp, prospects seemed distinctly good, as lions could be heard grunting in all directions.

Now this head of the expedition on a former visit, when I had the pleasure of accompanying him, was not at all taken with the African native cooks' style of cooking, and informed me, should he ever return, that he would certainly bring a Red Indian squaw. Evidently this did not materialise, although I did not see him on the next trip, when he met with fatal injuries.

It appears he was hunting lions one morning and about noon came up with a pride of them. Using a rifle of questionable merits, he fired at a maned lion, hitting it. The lion went down, apparently finished. Now here happened a terrible tragedy. Approaching this lion, the animal seemed to recover from its injuries, and the next moment was on top of him—man and lion in a terrible, desperate encounter. Eye-witnesses who were present informed me of the seemingly superhuman strength this man exerted. He fought the lion with his bare hands and practically succeeded in opening the jaws of the lion when they closed on him. The lion was killed, but not before several scratches and bites had been inflicted. The man's wife was in camp when the news of her injured husband was brought— surely a dreadful awakening. Arrangements were made to take the injured man to the doctor some distance away, and although medical attention was soon forthcoming, he gradually became worse and died, due to poisoning from the wounds inflicted. His body was cremated, and one sees the sad reality when one looks back over that tragic scene. The party leaving in high spirits, the leader a man over six feet high, a fine type of man, strong and fearless, and then this dreadful tragedy.

This will bring the danger home to anyone, never to approach a lion until you are assured he is dead.

I have seen dangerous animals lying still, evidently unconscious, only the white of the eye betraying life. It is in cases such as these that the animal is apt to recover and spring on you, before you realise the great danger involved.

A Pride of Lions

THE year 1922 found me hunting in that vast game crater Ngorongoro, in Tanganyika. There were animals literally in thousands, and I recollect so well hearing many lions grunting at all angles of the compass. One would imagine from the grunting sounds that the place was full of them, but these sounds can be very deceptive. These grand brutes could be easily heard three miles away, although to one unaccustomed they would appear to be one-third of this distance. During the night you could discern the short heavy grunts almost approaching a roar and gradually falling away to low successive notes.

I am of the opinion that the animals on which they prey are intimidated, or even hypnotised, by these calls all round them, which makes their prey an easy capture. I have often examined the scene of the actual catching or killing, and most frequently the rush has been short, and with the keen sense of vision and smell of the animal hunters they find themselves held by a superior spell when the actual stalk commences, and do not offer much resistance.

While hunting round a large swamp in this crater, named by the natives Toci-toc, I found the

spoor of a rhino which was comparatively fresh, and
was following it up when I imagined I heard a low
growl amongst some reeds about twenty yards on my
right. I stopped, and immediately a large bunch of
lions stood up and stared at me, sneaking off, grunting in displeasure. The master of this harem had a
splendid mane and I was sorely tempted to shoot,
only there were at least a dozen of them and they
were on the point of entering heavy reeds, so I
thought discretion the better part of valour, and
decided to try for him next day. Failing to come up
with the rhino, I made a large circuit back towards
camp, and in the distance in the open, near a
weather-beaten ant-hill, I espied an object which,
on getting closer, I saw was a lion. There was no
cover of any description on the plain, and I walked
towards it. Now the usual thing is that the lion
sees you before you see him, and this lion made no
attempt to clear off.

The native who accompanied me could not make
out his demeanour, and I suggested going closer.
It was interesting to watch this lion's movements.
When I took a step forward he crouched low, his
head on his paws, and on my moving to encircle
him he turned round and watched my every move.
It was obvious from the look of him that his bones
were fleshless, and here was a starving, famished
beast. In spite of my boys' entreaties, I refrained
from shooting him, as I wanted to see what he
would actually do. Having done a complete circle,
and he likewise on his own axis, I approached a few
yards closer. Now I saw him getting his hind legs

well pushed forward under him, and his miserable bony back arched up. He looked more like the Beggar of Beasts.

Next instant he threw up his tail and charged, but did not cover more than ten yards, when he returned to the spot he had sprung from, and sat down, eyeing me as before. I shot him, and found him to be the most miserable specimen of any lion I have ever shot. His teeth were broken down to discoloured stumps and his body one mass of mange, a smelling and vile beast. One could but picture the sight of that lion several years previously, hunting in all his massiveness, supplying food to the hyæna and vulture, and now reduced by age to humiliation, shortly to become the food of those he once befriended. I discovered that this old lion kept life together by following up herds of game and picking up any fallen offal.

A similar occurrence came to my notice in the Serengeti plains. Seeing a number of vultures and eagles hovering over a watercourse, I wended my way to find out the reason, when, approaching the place and peering over, I saw a mere skeleton of a lion sitting near a muddy mess. Putting up my rifle, I shot him where he lay, and then heard and saw much splashing in the mud he had been watching. On investigation, I found the mud was full of cat-fish, the brackish muddy water practically being dried up, and this lion was existing on this form of diet. Examination proved he had been previously wounded by a bullet in the hip joints, causing him the lack of strength to pull down any of the game feeding so close to him. So be it with the animal as well as the human race, which must remain the survival of the fittest.

To return to the crater Toci-toc, there were many prides of lions there which this old lion could have joined, but evidently the company of this old veteran was not sought.

Next day I was early on the scene in the direction of the pride I had disturbed the previous morning, and sitting down to listen, I could distinguish the low grunts of lions amongst the short " Baa " notes of the many wildebeests which were here in countless thousands. Sitting on a rock and watching these unbelievable herds of game, I saw my pride of the day before, sitting there on the plain, animals all round them, and taking not the slightest notice of the lions. It has often surprised me to see the confidence displayed between game and lion. These animals seem to know when the lions are hungry or otherwise. If it was the former, I do not think they would graze there in such close proximity, quite unconcerned. Such are the unwritten laws governing Nature and its instincts.

As the sun rose higher I could see my pride of this pride, standing up surveying the landscape all round, and I knew they would soon head for the edge of the reeds, the cover of which affords wonderful shade from the midday sun. He was then joined by the others, who commenced walking slowly in my direction. Now this was a formidable band, consisting of one lord and nine ladies of the veldt, and I then realised they would

H

enter the thick belt of cover further along, ahead of me.

Seeing a small isolated clump of reeds fifty yards ahead, I commenced crawling on my belly and reached it without being seen. There was safety in this method. When I did shoot, even if the others did not connect the exact place the report came from, the mob would not attempt to take the small piece of cover, but would bolt for safety to the main reed bed. Watching them coming slowly forward, just like a number of dogs, was interesting, with the old majestic fellow bringing up the rear. When within forty yards of my cover, they all sat down, and turned their faces to the vast herds of game gambolling in front.

I watched a lioness brush past the old maned gentleman, who looked to me the essence of happiness and purred in content. I would have liked a picture of this happy family group, who would a few minutes later receive a rude awakening. A vulture flew low over my abode where I sat and swerved off, and immediately I saw the lions look at the clump, such is their marvellous instinct of danger.

In all walks of big game hunting, bird life invariably plays an important part, which the animal instinctively accepts, and it warns him of immediate or approaching danger. The lions now commenced moving off, and passed my ambush at twenty yards. Pushing the outside fringe of the reeds aside with the barrel of my rifle, the lion saw this slight movement immediately and stood for a second, while the rest continued walking. I fired at his chest. He reeled, and fell on the ground, growling savagely. Two of the lionesses—one of them a very light fawn colour, which I had seen making advances to him a few minutes earlier—tore back to where he lay and stood there—the very essence of defiance. I am sure had I shown myself she would have charged instanter, as they went through all the antics governing a charge, but could not find the one to vent their feelings on. They stayed beside him for at least five minutes before stealing off in the direction the others had taken, when man, the destroyer, ventured forth to claim the coveted trophy.

I spent ten days in one territory before I came up with a trio of fine maned lions (beasts that had been doing a lot of damage among cattle), and yet I tried all the cunning I knew during this period in order to bag them. They lived in impenetrable bush, which was nearly a mile long, and never did they venture from this thicket until after nightfall. I have heard it said that manes of this fine type are never found in thorn bush, as the bush destroys and pulls out the hair. This I have found is not so— black maned lions may suddenly turn up in any part, be the altitude 4,000 feet or double this figure. I am willing to admit that the colder climates do produce the majority, as you find him with a fuller mane which comes back to his flank.

Within the past year, when hunting near the Duma watercourse in Tanganyika Territory, I saw several fine-maned lions in one morning between 6.30 and 9 a.m. These comprised a group of two

and three and two single ones, one of the latter
exceptional. I was returning through some open
mimosa bush and saw something which looked like
a black burnt tree stump. Stopping the automobile,
I made certain with my glasses, and here was one of
the finest lions I have yet seen. When he moved
his massive head you could discern his other
features. He looked so grand sitting there, I did
not want to disturb him.

I had seen a picture of a similar lion, showing
masses of mane on the belly, and was interested to
see if our African lion grew such, as out of several
thousands I have seen, this was the most imposing.
Taking the automobile near him and pressing the
electric horn, I made a din and yet he did not seem
disturbed by this strange sound of the veldt. Getting the wind of the lorry, he stood up, a magnificent
sight, and his belly was smooth, similar to all the
others I have seen. I then realised that I had been
hoaxed by the American-born lion, and the wonderful lion depicted with mane below—which at the
time I admired—had been taken from a cage, and
was a tame one.

It may interest many readers to know that lions
in captivity grow much finer and heavier manes
than those found on the African plains. In parts
of the world today there are lion farms, where
wonderful specimens are bred, reared, and may be
hired to stage animal pictures.

My lion of the veldt was a credit to his name, and
I am certain his setting, roaming in the frame of
Africa's gilt picture, would take a better-gifted pen

than mine to describe. I have touched too lightly on the scene to do him justice. These vast plains, far from the pale or trend of man, are a wonderful sanctuary for such splendid beasts. It is well, for they could never be adapted to any other purpose. The soil is poor, the water bad, and Nature has evidently so ordained it that under the trust of their only enemy—man—fauna will live and flourish.

I apologise to my readers for leaving the spoor of the marauders I was hunting. I placed bait for them in the way of a dead zebra and opened it, to make the attraction better. It was partaken of, and at daybreak no sign of them. I altered the menu by tying a wildebeest, hartebeest and zebra together, and the same thing happened. Waiting by night, I listened to this trio emitting their magnificent volume of sound. One of them always seemed to have a pronounced rolling of his notes when taking his part. The second night I waited in vain. They circled me and went off at a lumbering gallop, letting off " whoofy " grunts. This puzzled me, and I was wont to imagine myself beaten.

From the lay of the land and the fact that I had fed these lions for eight days and not a whit nearer, I formed a plan which eventually did bring me face to face with them. The bush where I had baited these beasts was near a ravine, the head water or commencement being at least half a mile away from the main donga, where it tapered out to a few isolated trees towards the plain. Here was my plan, which became their undoing. That morning the meat of these partly putrid carcases was dragged up the edge of the ravine to the uppermost cover, which was composed of a few stunted mimosa thorns.

The kill was now arranged with the utmost care, and the meat tied to the base of a bush with wire to prevent them picking it up and carrying it away. In the early part of the evening it rained heavily. This was all in my favour on account of the smell of humans being washed away, and again, rain after a period of drought gives these big cats confidence, and they may forget their antagonists for the time being. That night, the lions gave vent to their lungs properly, and it is probably well known that lions give tongue or throat more during the early part of the rains than at any other time. The smell and feel of the rain would take them out, as the constant drip of rain in heavy bush does not appeal to them.

Next morning my old Masai warrior, my trusted tracker, came along to my tent to say the lions were grunting near the kill, but I had already been listening to their music for some time past. Hurriedly dressing, and partaking of a frugal meal, we set off towards the heavy bush, and if there is one thing unpleasant in Africa, it is walking in the dark. If there is a stone, bush, or any obstacle on the way, you seem to run foul of it. Arriving at the bottom of the donga, it was real good news to hear the low satisfied grunts at the top of it, the only obstacle being darkness, and when waiting for dawn to break it appears to take so long to come. When the first streak of dawn appeared on the horizon, it was most welcome, and we commenced walking up the ravine towards the bait, myself taking the left side, while the tracker cut through to the opposite side, and followed up parallel with me, lest they might return by that way and not be seen.

Some distance up, where the ravine came to a narrow neck, we rejoined and could then easily negotiate either side if need be. Between here and the kill we spotted, in fact we all saw at the same time, that the lions were cut off. From their attitude it was evident they were determined to charge down on us, for their haven of retreat in the valley below. Two of these lions had splendid manes, and I fired at the largest one, which was standing on the left side next to the plain. He went down on his chest—I had evidently hit him too low— and the noise he created was horrible to hear. The others did not hesitate and came down that incline at a speed I would not have credited. Shooting at the leader, I hit him right in the centre of the throat and he turned a somersault. The third lion at this gave one tremendous roar and leapt into the narrow gorge and beat it properly. This is the one and only time that I have seen a lion beat it, with his tail tucked tight behind him. That this lion charged for safety and won it, there could be no disputing, although when I was engaged with number two, he could have made it awkward had he preferred. These two lions were old, but in splendid condition, the measurements unskinned being 9 feet 8 inches and 9 feet 4 inches. It had taken patience and time to get up with these crafty animals, but here was man's craft pitted against animals' cunning, the chances being more or less equal.

Duncan routs a Trio

A FEW years ago an amusing, but extremely foolhardy, incident happened in that desolate region, the Northern Frontier Province in Kenya. On this particular trip I was hunting with a Montreal sportsman, Duncan McMartin. Now Duncan is one of these sporting fellows, afraid of nothing, and the more excitement the better he likes it. The beginning of our hunt was securing different species of trophies to ornament his Canadian home. During this trip large and un-hunted areas were visited, and in course of time the game bag was being filled with choice specimens. In that bleak and barren spot, Lasamis, there are several water-holes where rhinos are practically compelled to drink, on account of the scarcity of water in the surrounding area, and nine bleached rhino skulls which my porters placed in a row near my tent bore testimony to the numbers which have been killed at this spot.

While watching sand grouse coming to drink in their countless numbers, two of these sullen, morose beasts came slowly down over the white dusty brow to slake their thirst. Here are the remains of stone hides or huts which have been used either to photo-graph or kill these animals, maybe partaking of their last drink. When the water in several pools reaches a low ebb, and access is only gained through channels of rocks, several of these animals have actually found themselves wedged and practically held as in a vice, and immediately they find themselves gripped they try to push on through, instead of backing out. Here would be a splendid chance to use dynamite and prevent a recurrence. Shooting a rhino there was easy. Many good horns have been taken from this locality, and it would be interesting to know how many animals have been killed here during the past thirty years.

Our next camp was on the borders of the Northern Game Reserve, and an interesting place. During the course of our stay much game, both big and small, was seen. Spotting a solitary bull buffalo, we managed to creep up behind some cover, and as he was feeding towards us, he was allowed to come on. While we waited, he came slowly on, head down and browsing in his stride. All eyes were intent on this beast, when in the next second we had a rude awakening. A large rhino cow, accompanied by her youngster, which was nearly as large as herself, came tearing straight at us from behind. Duncan loosed off and that rhino bit the dust. The young one, which had several inches of horn, stood there puffing and letting off steam like an old one. As we did not want to kill it, we moved off in the direction we had seen our buffalo. Now not a sign of him—he had made good his escape when the rhino charged.

Waiting for an hour or so, we resolved to try and drive the young one away. It was at least a year past the milk stage, and there was no reason why it should not connect up with others, as there were many in this district. Returning to the carcase, we threw a stone which hit it, and it did a large circle round us and then headed straight into the Game Reserve. While examining our unwanted trophy, we noticed the spoor of several lions, and here was an ideal kill under good conditions, as the low bush would enable us to stalk up to it without being seen.

Turkana natives, who lived in this district, informed us that the lions here were very big and had attacked several of their camels a few days previously. These members of the Turkana tribe looked a warlike lot, the men having steel spikes in their lips and sharp cutting knives encircled on their wrists. Their wives' heads were ornamented with cemented mud and massed shells. My friend was puzzled as to how the men embraced them, with these terrible cutting devices. Leaving the camp next morning, we strolled in the direction of the rhino carcase. About half-way, when passing some thorn bush, we heard a sort of purring growl, and to our surprise three magnificent black-maned lions bolted close from beside us. And then we noticed they had killed the young rhino we had spared the previous day. Quick as a flash they bolted, and Duncan, nearly as quick, raced after them. I was just too surprised, but gazed on the scene. There were three of the finest lions I had ever seen, and Duncan behind them shooting as he ran. These lions never looked back, they must have known by instinct he was no friend, but they kept on heading for that boundary which would give them safety, the

Game Reserve. Twice when Duncan shot I heard the grunt of the lion and the " flup " of the bullet.

Following in the trail Duncan had taken, I came upon him at least half a mile away. He was standing over a beautiful black-maned beast. I enquired where the others had gone and was informed he had lost sight, after shooting at them. Here was sorrow ! I knew these lions would not return, and they did not. Retracing our steps back towards the rhino they had killed, we evidently took a short cut, and here, to our great surprise, was another lion, quite dead, one only from this great trio being left to tell the tale.

It was indeed most exceptional to see such imposing beasts, especially in one troop. Evidently they hunted together, and from the marks on the earth beside that rhino it must have been a terrible encounter. The ground was dug up and stones uplifted as the rhino had made repeated charges before being pulled down. The back was lacerated with deep gashes and it was evident from the position of the body that they forced it down, attacking its throat. This is the only occasion I have seen a rhino killed by lion. They must have killed it for the love of killing, as had they wanted to gorge there was the large one, already slit open for invitation, or it may have been that the younger one returned to guard its mother, and, finding the lions near by, gave battle with dire results.

Returning from here, we saw many herds of animals moving off, evidently in the direction of the smell of rain. I have heard the word " migration " used regarding our game, but think " movement " would be more applicable, as our animals in Eastern Africa only move from one plain to another, or in places like the vast Serengetti in Tanganyika, they move from one end to the other, as showers have fallen and pasture with its forced growth attracts accordingly. I have watched vast herds of thousands of animals of many species —particularly wildebeest and zebra—trekking off, but they simply move with the rains and feeding, and never leave the main areas.

It may be asked, " Are not lions dangerous in the open plains ?" In daylight I say " No," and the same will apply to all our so-called dangerous game. The general rule is, although there may be the infrequent exception, that all our dangerous animals in the open will, and do, give way to man or womankind. It is only when the animal is hunted, wounded, or hustled, and gets into cover, that no liberty can be taken. Personally, I would rather cross a plain full of buffalo in Africa than a field in Scotland in which there was a domestic bull. I have done both, and speak from experience

I trust these remarks will not detract from the main issue—thrills. There are many thrills awaiting those who seek, but you can spend years in the bush without encountering one. The sporting blood of mankind will ever seek for such, and beard these animals in their dens to attain it. Yea, I have seen men—I may also be guilty—you find yourself amongst a herd of dangerous game, you become one of themselves without fear of being in danger, and not one whit better than the determined charging buffalo, which only death can stop.

CHAPTER TWELVE

Lions in the Kitchen

DURING the year 1927, a companion and myself arranged to carry out an expedition which would cover a march from south of Lake Victoria to the centre of the best game country in the interior. Our forty porters, mostly of the Kavirondo tribe, were recruited at Kibigori station.

Expecting to be off the beaten track for some time, a considerable amount of tinned provisions was taken, also a quantity of ground maize for the porters, which was rationed out at the rate of 2 lb. per person daily. There was the possibility of shooting buck of some description for them on the way to eke out this meal, the porterage of which was considerable. It was a great day when we set off into the blue, the natives all replete in new blankets, a change from the grimy rags they had previously worn, going off with their loads and singing in high glee.

During the first two days we struck westwards into the Kisii district, passing *en route* many native shambas and villages. After leaving this area, we headed southwards, which in four days would take us into the Uasin Gishu Masai area. The Masai had moved there from the Eldama ravine district a few years earlier, when they had been given land in exchange for that taken over by European settlers. During this march we encountered much rain, and the singing of our native porters gave way to gloominess. We trudged on still southwards, and when west of the Lumbwa district, several of our porters deserted, leaving their loads in the grass. They were disgruntled because they wanted meat, and during a week's march we had not seen the signs of one herd of game. Many disused game pits were passed, proving that the animal world was represented at one time, but had evidently been hunted and killed by these natives many years previous.

On the fifth day we were short of more porters, and the chop-boxes which contained our provisions had been thrown away. I knew they had fled back to their villages. This was certainly annoying, as there were no other porters to be recruited *en route* to replace them. With promises of elephant meat and salt (this is their weakness) to the remainder of the gang, we continued our journey. A three-days trek would bring us into elephant country, when the natives could eat meat to their heart's content.

West of Manga, on the eastern fringe of the Masai country, were many undulating grass-topped hills, and here were many bohor reed-buck and oribi. Camping for one day, I scouted round and shot three of these animals. It was evident from their tameness they had not been previously hunted. This change of diet entirely altered the temperament of the porters, and they were now looking forward to elephant meat, as the half-caste Masai who lived here mentioned there were many elephants in the district.

My companion had never up to this time seen an elephant, and I was bombarded daily with an array of questions where to shoot them and where not. Getting fed up, I told him to shoot as he would a kongoni (one of the hartebeest family), and he did so later.

Camping in an area between the Masai and Jaluo tribes, we soon had news of elephants from both parties; from the former, with a view to backsheesh, and from the Jaluo from their love of meat.

The Masai will not partake of elephant flesh, but their capacity for beef is incredible. It is the custom of several of these young Masai warriors to clear off from their kraals accompanied by young girls of ten years of age, taking with them an ox. They will then find the most inaccessible places, where they are not likely to be discovered, and killing the ox, have a regular " beano " for several days, returning to their kraal when the meat is finished. It is not infrequent for each member of his company to account for 20 lb. of beef at one sitting. These meetings are not encouraged by Government, but in my wanderings I have come on at least a score of them. Their temporary home is generally made in the thickest bush, the entrance being heavily covered with thorns. The method adopted in killing the animal is shooting an arrow into a vein, when they collect the blood in gourds, and on completion, spear the weakened ox.

Eight elephant bulls were reported in our vicinity, and in the afternoon we journeyed to look for them. At five o'clock we came on their tracks leading into a ravine, which we followed for a mile, when we could hear these animals feeding. The sound of breaking branches made them appear closer than they were.

Approaching with the greatest caution, my friend was now excited beyond words, eager to get a glimpse of them. He did not have long to wait, I heard the low guttural throaty sound of one, and the next instant they came crashing down the ravine and stopped only thirty yards from us, listening towards the direction from which they had come. The wind being in our favour, I could not understand the cause of their alarm, afterwards discovering they had been frightened at meeting a rhino. My friend, while waiting trying to get a glimpse of their ivory, which at this time was valued at £1 for a pound, declared it was not worth it, and pleaded to get out of the bush. He broke a rotten stick, and the noise set the already disturbed elephants off once more, passing us without notice at a distance of only a few feet. How they did not run us down I do not know. Their great size seemed to use up all available space in the ravine.

Getting to the edge of the bush, we ran down a trail, and to our surprise these elephants were all standing bunched together as if in prayer. There was one large bull amongst the lot, but he was practically covered by the bodies of the others, and

Refusing to leave his comrade. This sad scene took place near Kasigau Hill in Kenya. A grief-stricken young bull refused to leave his fallen pal, a monarch that carried 240 pounds of ivory.

River scene, Northern Rhodesia. The thatch-roofed canoe is regularly used on the Chambezi, which empties into Lake Bangweolo, Northern Rhodesia. It is the native passenger service between villages on that beautiful river.

"I fear no foe," this fine black-maned lion seems to say. The zebra bait in the foreground we dragged by lorry toward this black-maned lion. He promptly took possession, grunting disapproval at being photographed.

The author.

Close range. The elephant depicted carried tusks weighing seventy pounds apiece. When wind is against them and they face the sun, these animals may be approached to within ten yards in bush country.

Lunch in the shade.

Lioness scanning the veldt. On the numerous kopjes in the Serengetti plains, Tanganyika, lions are specially prone to rest during the midday heat.

A lioness posing. Lions are not natural climbers: By a well-timed spring, however, coupled with the dexterous use of her powerful claws, she attained her objective.

The buffalo spotted us. On the Soda Flats of Lake Natron, Kenya. Denys Finch Hatton and myself, our backs camouflaged with reeds, wormed our way to within thirty-five yards of these African bovines.

Puku near Lake Rukwa, Tanganyika. These graceful, reddish-yellow antelope are most numerous on the adjoining flats of Lake Rukwa. They are easily approached and show little alarm at being photographed.

Carrion eaters. Vultures waiting in the background for lions to leave their kill. These birds are a constant menace to carnivores, and soon devour any kill left unguarded.

Hunter and sportsman. The late Hon. Denys Finch Hatton, one of the bravest hunters I have ever met, and in whose death I lost a pal.

A bull giraffe ruminating. The tallest of all mammals, the giraffe has few enemies and is a constant attraction to photographers. In recent years they have become increasingly tame.

Coveted trophies. The hunter's antelope, found only in the Tanaland and Jubaland provinces, are still plentiful and remain an attraction for the collecting sportsman.

Morose and sullen. These ponderous creatures, dour but agile, are plentiful in several parts of Kenya and Tanganyika. Away from the beaten track, up to a dozen rhino may be seen in a day's trek.

Cruel killers. Wild dogs are the cruelest foes of African fauna. Their staying power is exceptional, and the hunted antelope that soon loses heart falls an easy victim.

my friend was confident the remainder were hiding him. We decided to approach closer by traversing a piece of marshy ground, and of course, the worst would happen. My friend, in picking the barest places, went up to his middle in a morass, yelling for me to help him. It looked too ridiculous—the elephants on one side, and the hunter bogged within fifty yards of them. This was too much for the elephants, they listened for a second, then floundered—all their weight against them—through the mud with ease. Shooting the big one was one of the ordeals of my life. He looked so easy, but in the swamp it was well-nigh impossible to get your feet in a suitable position to fire the heavy rifles from. We both breathed a sigh of relief when that fine tusker sank in the mud, dying in an upright position, fore-feet and tusks supporting him as if alive.

The tusks of this elephant were cut out with the greatest difficulty, and scaled 86 and 90 lb. respectively.

Securing this trophy, the next move on the programme was to shoot two lions. Our safari trekked south-east a further sixty miles, occupying five days. Our porters had gorged on elephant meat and were now quite reconciled to the general routine of safari life. On the way we saw a certain amount of game, chiefly water-buck, topi, and hartebeest.

Hunting in the Chipulungu forest, we ran foul of a large herd of elephants, which appeared to be mostly cows, and on account of the soft clay type

I

of ground we had some difficulty in extricating ourselves. After our previous experience, my friend did not wish to adopt closer acquaintanceship; he now intensely disliked elephants, and our forest hunt for some of the rarer antelopes quickly terminated.

Continuing our trip to the open plains country to the south was easy going. From where we camped that night, lions could be heard in the distance. Next morning we were early astir and moved down the escarpment towards the direction of the magic notes. That afternoon we wandered past a wooded watercourse and at the extreme end I spotted a tawny object sitting near some bush on the left bank. Taking the cover of the banks of the dongo, we walked quietly down, my friend saying he must shoot his first lion. At sixty yards range we passed over the low embankment, and there, reposing in the sunset, sitting like a dog, was a fine tawny-maned lion. My friend was using a ·318 Westley Richards rifle, and placing his helmet on the ground, and using it as a rest, lay at the prone position. I don't know how long he aimed, but I thought he would never fire, and the lion looked in the opposite direction, quite unsuspecting. At the report the lion in view jumped up and cleared off immediately.

While my friend was blaming the rifle (as he could not have missed it, but I am always dubious of the sport who dwells on his aim), the most extraordinary thing happened. There was deep breathing behind the bush, the heavy sighs which only the king of beasts can do, and on our investigating, there lay one of the finest dark-maned lions I have ever seen, shot through the neck. My friend's rifle was now transformed into the most accurate weapon known, and here was a beautiful shot. He had not seen this lion when he fired. Some people, they say, are born lucky shots. I will sidetrack my narrative to illustrate.

Two sportsmen were marching along the dusty highway near Lake Rukwa, Nature's paradise on the western side of Tanganyika. They both carried rifles, and nearing camp some puku antelopes were seen grazing within a hundred yards from the road. Thinking he might miss, the visitor asked the other sport to take the shot, which he did, remarking, as the puku dropped, " I always shoot them through the heart." The visitor was much impressed by such accurate shooting, but on examining the animal, he exclaimed, " Hey, I did not know the puku carried his heart in his skull !" My readers will realise there is a gap here of at least two feet between.

Returning to our lion hunt, my friend was in luck's way, and the manner his lion died was re-told several times, making it appear a good shot instead of a lucky one.

Our next camp was arranged on a ridge overlooking vast plains to the north and east. As far as the eye could scan, game were to be seen singly and in masses. There were many small ravines within easy reach of our camp, and at night lions grunted from each of them. While camped there, my friend shot an impala ram for food, which was brought to the camp and hung up in the kitchen. I would mention that the latter comprised a tarpaulin thrown over some cross members, a few large stones to make the fireplace, coupled with a few chop-boxes, which completed the outfit.

In the absence of rains, porters usually make their grass beds on the earth near the fire, the heavens their roof. My friend and self were occupying a tent nearby. At nine o'clock that night, the cook, having finished baking bread for the morrow, suddenly realised two lions sneaking up on him. Without further ado, he streaked his fastest into our tent, his corduroy trousers giving vent to their rubbing as he ran. Standing between our beds, I am sure he was on the point of trying to get underneath. Yairo—that was his name— stood there, lips and mouth moving, but not one word escaping. We saw he was scared out of his senses, and on my friend flashing his torch there were two fully grown lionesses in the kitchen under the tarpaulin, and in possession of our larder. I rushed out and had the satisfaction of seeing them carrying off our impala, giving low growls as they moved off. My friend wanted to teach the thieves a lesson, but as one of them showed a maternal bearing, we let them have our meat.

While we remained in that camp, these lions used to prowl nightly all round the tents, but never attempted to molest us. It may be that should any of you ever visit that camp, their cubs will also welcome you.

Buffalo

IN this year as I write the general reader may probably imagine that with these passing years of civilisation, coupled with the latest in death-dealing rifles, the game in Africa is being depleted. So much so that National Game Parks and complete portions of Africa for the reservation of the African fauna have been urged, and advocated. The idea is indeed good, but if some of these critics would actually come out to Africa and see the vast quantities of game as it stands, the minds of their followers would be eased and a different complex shown.

Compared with ten years ago, the actual killing today has been in my opinion reduced by 60 per cent. Photography has in many cases super-seded the rifle, and pictures taken against trophies seized with the rifle. Where lions a few years ago were shot, irrespective of numbers, today they offer endless amusement by your driving up to them in an automobile and taking photographs in place of their hides. When a few years ago it was difficult to shoot them on foot, today the automobile has entirely reversed the situation. You can take the car up to them—they will even eat by it, sleep, and mate by it. Such is their contempt for a car, that so long as they do not see mankind's legs dangling from it, or standing on it, they are easier to approach than any antelope.

Again, it may interest the world to learn that the best show of game in Africa is not to be seen in the Game Reserves, but to be seen on Crown land which is accessible to the visitor. This in itself will show that our African fauna is still at a high level, and the law of Nature must in time assert itself in combating overstocking our best centres. Then there is the grave risk of inbreeding amongst the smaller antelopes, whose numbers run into countless thousands in several areas. Take, for example, the red letchwe on those great Kaful flats in Northern Rhodesia. Amongst these unbelievable numbers will be seen undersized puny creatures, freak females carrying malformed horns, in my opinion the direct result of inbreeding. (The reader should understand that female letchwe do not carry horns.)

With these remarks I will now take my readers on to more of our dangerous beasts. The buffalo is in my opinion one of the most formidable and dangerous animals to be reckoned with in Africa today. Here you have an antagonist imbued with all the cunning and ferocity which it is possible to imagine, his sense of hearing, smell and indomitable courage being unsurpassed. Having hunted these daring animals in five different countries in Africa, I can honestly say I hold him in great respect, and know of no more determined animal, especially when wounded and in cover to his liking. That I lost two of the best trackers I ever possessed through them still adds to the lustre of his bravery, and as long as men hunt him, so the buffalo will continue to take his toll. His is a fight to the finish, and not until his adversary is one mangled mass is he content to leave him. That terrible grunt as he strikes each blow shows his whole weight behind it. His hoofs, both fore and aft, stamping and trouncing with maddened fury on the unfortunate victim, can better be left to your own imagination.

My old Masai warrior—my trusted tracker— referred to above, is today at rest, from the onslaught of an infuriated buffalo, but I avenged him. We had hunted for years together, and will I ever forget his smile of contentment when he saw that great black hulk, his adversary, lying dead? Our hunts confronted me—all too vivid—and now his last hunt. Was I weak if I sat down and wept?

Buffalo are found in most of the forest belts in Africa today and I am of the opinion are steadily increasing numerically. The greatest numbers are to be found in Tanganyika Territory and Mozambique, Portuguese East Africa. The largest herd of these animals I have seen was near the Rufigi River, and I place the numbers at a mean estimate of seven hundred. On the plains in Mozambique as I write herds are very numerous, many of them reaching three or four hundred.

I should say that the best heads are obtained in the southern Masai area in Kenya, where heads of fifty-one inch spread are not uncommon. In the last mentioned I have found the bulls most aggressive, and liable to attack without being hunted. My readers will picture in their minds meeting one of these formidable adversaries, ever inquisitive, nose stretched forward and the sullen eyes taking in your every movement.

When following a wounded animal, the greatest care must be taken, otherwise unnecessary risks must end in disaster to the hunter. He has a habit of leaving his trail, doing a half-circle and waiting until you pass, when he will take you from behind, and only his death will save you.

The lion, when he mauls you, may still leave you life, not so the buffalo. His satisfaction is only complete when he has trampled the last breath out of you. His swimming powers are truly remarkable, and there are instances where these animals have actually been seen swimming from islands in the Bukakata group in Lake Victoria to the mainland, a feat which seems incredible. There was a buffalo attacked by crocodiles while swimming across and natives with spears waiting to attack immediately he reached shore, and even with this the natives did not have the best of it.

I have shot the red buffalo in the Semliki valley, but they appear to be a meridian type and quite different from the Congo dwarf species, as the horns are like miniatures of the ordinary black variety. I remember on one occasion hunting buffalo in that splendid area near Lake Edward in Uganda, and a large herd was spotted in a valley, comprising over one hundred beasts. Amongst them I noticed two red buffalo, and I played a long game in stalking them before shooting the pair, which were both cows and similar to those I secured in the Semliki.

Having hunted in both of these areas, I was satisfied that the Congo dwarf buffalo did not come further east than the fringe of the Ituri forest in the Congo Belge. In the latter forest, there were many of them ranging in herds up to fifty or more in each. I was interested in this snappy sporting type. They are not built on the clumsy side, compared to the black variety. Their flattened, scarcely curved horns, tufted ears and large eyes, combined with sleek coats, make them an enviable trophy. The meat I found to be very palatable. As a rule, they only emerge from the forest and feed in the lanes, approaching the native shambas in the late dusk.

I made a hide, ensconced myself and watched them on two occasions feed close under the tree in which I was in hiding. The cows were a fawn colour, while the bulls usually bringing up the rear were a rusty chestnut shade. They feed up to the native gardens and eat sweet potato leaves. Many are under the impression that this animal is more ferocious than his black brother. I can assert that this is not so, and he is much easier stopped than the latter. They are very partial to visiting salt licks and take a great liking to wallowing in mud, as do the other variety.

In one area of the great Ituri forest I am sure there exist many thousands of them. The natives kill many of them by pitfalls and suspended spear traps. These wary animals are quite alive to the cunningly devised engines which are laid and set with great dexterity. Many times I have visited these set traps and it is interesting to see how the animals know how to jump free of the pits and evade the snare. The natives' success depends mostly on stampeding and driving the animals in headlong flight amongst them.

The natives in this place are not allowed rifles, as in many other parts, which is all in the interests of these fine animals, and I trust it will remain so. The privilege allowed to natives in having rifles to protect their crops is so frequently abused, and I do not see that any department can ever keep a check on their killings. In the backwoods and many near woods in Africa, the natives are inveterate meat-eaters, and they would never think of killing one of their stock for consumption, as long as a bony or juicy antelope lived in their neighbourhood.

Returning to our black buffalo, I have had many thrilling times with these sporting and ferocious animals, and will relate a few of my encounters.

I accompanied a lady visitor who was keen to bag one of these trophies, and we set off one afternoon about 4 p.m., to hunt round some low bush adjoining a large swamp. Now buffalo usually commence to feed in the late afternoon, and as this time of the day is usually cool, hunting can be pleasant. Within a mile we spotted a single bull ahead of us, and keeping him in view as far as possible, hurried on in his direction. Where we last saw him, there was lots of spoor from other buffalo feeding in the bush adjoining, and the bush seemed full of buffalo just ahead of us.

We had not moved far when the outline of a black object was seen standing. I peered forward, but could not make out if it was our bull or not. Kneeling down, I noticed it was a buffalo cow and she had evidently just given birth to a calf. I could distinctly see the little calf, dark red in colour, trying to stand and falling down again, while the mother, standing over it, licked it all over.

Evidently she heard or smelt us, and the next instant she left her calf and charged in our direction, but finding herself getting away from the newly-born, much to our relief, she turned round and rushed back to the calf. Doing a retreat backwards for some little distance until we were out of her way, we soon were on the fringe of the thicket, and on continuing on I heard a heavy gallop and rush behind, and here was the old bull we had previously hunted bearing down straight on us with head lowered, tail straight up, a really blood-curdling sight. He was shot in the base of the neck where it joins the shoulders and went spread-eagled on his belly, bellowing as he crashed at three yards behind us, the impetus of his rush having carried him on for some distance after being hit.

Now here was a charge from an unprovoked beast, apart from the fact that we were on his ground.

From that day onwards I have always had the corner of my eye—in thick bush—keeping an outlook to the rear. There is nothing like practical experience to make yourself adaptable.

During my experiences I have found the herd bull to be more vindictive than the older animal; perhaps the latter's hearing and vision are not so keen. Buffalo cows, unless accompanied by a young calf, I have never found troublesome, although on one occasion I came on four cows standing in some fairly open ground, and on my passing by them, one of them charged me. I did not realise until afterwards that she was in the first throes of that fell disease, rinderpest (the cholera of the veldt), otherwise she would not have done so. Even when following a wounded cow buffalo in heavy bush, I have seen her break away, when had it been a bull, the common result would have happened.

Hunting in that portion to which I have already made reference, where the largest buffalo heads were taken from, I was accompanied by a native tracker whose only raiment was a cotton blanket, twisted round his loins, and we followed up a narrow ravine for at least a mile. A single buffalo bull crashed forward and tore up the gully. Further in we espied him leaving it and taking refuge in an isolated clump of bush which was near the ravine.

I was armed with a double Express rifle, while my tracker carried a Mauser 9·3 m.m. rifle. Cautiously approaching and walking along without looking at the bush lest he would catch our eye and bolt, I sent my tracker round to the plains side of the bush and instructed him to heave in some stones, which would drive the bull my way, as I was intercepting him from the donga. The native getting round did so, and at his second throw out came that buffalo at him. Before he even realised what was happening, it was on him, and with the first sweep of its massive horns, which I later measured fifty-three inches, it took the blanket in its thrust from the boy's body and commenced goring it, the barrel of the rifle he carried being bent round like a hoop, such was the force of his onset. One shot in the point of the shoulder and he sank, receiving a second in the chest before he could recover. I am of the opinion that it was probably on account of the old dark red blanket the boy carried which made it charge in his direction; it was exceptional for it to charge at him in the open air and on a gradient, or it may have been from sheer cussedness.

In the Southern Congo a friend and myself were elephant hunting, and one evening we spotted a large herd of buffalo feeding on an open patch adjoining a narrow strip of tall reeds. We commenced crawling up to them and before long could hear them grazing and emitting short notes, not unlike that of domestic cattle. Within seventy yards we managed to sneak upon the herd, which spotted us, and being curious, they walked a few steps towards us. My friend was quite certain they were going to charge, not knowing their idle curiosity when they see human beings for the first time. Spotting the largest bull, we decided to take him, and fired. At the first shot the whole herd stampeded, the dust raised making it impossible to get another shot. They immediately bolted across the line of reeds, and galloped across to the other side.

My friend in the meantime wanted to be after them, but I restrained him from doing so, as I could not understand how the wounded animal could be keeping up with the main herd, and suspected his waiting in the reeds, my friend being certain that he had passed through. Knowing their cunning, we walked over to within twenty yards of the reeds, and while I threw in stones my friend waited to shoot. No sign—not a sound—and my second was now absolutely satisfied the path was clear. I insisted on three more throws, and at my second effort there was a crash. My piece of rock hit him right in the palm of his horn. He tore out, the picture of fury, foaming at the mouth, and came straight at us, with that curious twisting gait, grunting hoarsely as he charged. My friend shot him, and from the double report I am convinced to this day he pulled both triggers together, two bullets entering the forehead from the eye, killing him instantly.

This will give you an idea as to their cunning, and but for that stone hitting him, he would have waited and charged us immediately, we being at a disadvantage in the bush, and the majority in his favour. There is always a great danger when shooting him in bush, on account of the bullet hitting numerous branches and twigs, in some cases deflecting the bullet and destroying the accuracy and striking power of your missile. This is one of the big items in favour of your adversary, and I am of the opinion that many a European's death has been attributable to this last cause.

CHAPTER FOURTEEN

Filming Buffalo Herds

BUFFALO meat as a rule is coarse and tough, the two extremes—his tail and tongue—providing the best part. When buffalo shooting, only solid bullets should be used (insurance agents should insist), and the rifle which gives the most shocking and striking power you are capable of using will not be found too heavy. It may interest many of my readers to know that the look of some heavy Express rifles is apt to scare the visitor (perhaps most so the enormous cartridges), on account of the recoil when fired. On firing at a target you think of the recoil that is coming—then, of course, you feel it; but when you are shooting at big game you feel no recoil, all this being taken up on excitement, thrill, possession, or anything you like to call it. On three occasions, when escorting ladies, I have put my heavy ·450 No. 2 rifle (which shoots 80 grains of cordite and a 480-grain bullet, and weighs 10½ lb.) into their hands; they fire, and in absence of recoil remark, "I thought these big guns kicked." This will show that a woman can shoot any rifle made when she is up against dangerous game.

Only once have I been caught in a stampeding herd of buffaloes, and I do not wish ever to be in a similar predicament. It happened in this way.

Fourteen years ago I was attached to a party who were hunting greater kudu, that beautiful antelope, near the Ngaruka hills, which lie midway between Arusha and Ngorogoro crater, in Tanganyika Territory. Early one morning we left the flats and scouted on the small plateaux adjoining some foot-hills.

I was accompanied by a remarkably fine old Dutch hunter, a man who knew this country thoroughly, having hunted there when the territory belonged to Germany. Scanning the country, my hunter friend spotted a herd of buffalo; there appeared to be altogether a hundred animals. I was keen on securing a couple of good buffalo heads and off we set in their direction. They were all lying down in an open glade within sixty yards of a wooded ravine. We made a detour to avoid giving them the wind and slowly but surely reached a point where we could with certainty pick out the heads required.

Rinderpest was then troublesome in the area, but from what we could see this herd appeared perfectly healthy. We were now slightly below the herd, and selecting the two largest bulls which were lying down, opened fire. At the report of our rifles the whole herd stood, milled round in a circle, and the next instant the entire herd started coming in our direction. They simply raced in one terrible rush, a mad stampede, each trying to get ahead of the other. My Dutch hunter called to me to take a tree quickly, and I just managed to clamber up the bent trunk of a tree—in fact, was barely clear

—when that panic-striken massed herd, looking neither to the right nor left, crashed down on us, rushing headlong on even with their short rush, a sweating and streaming mob. After they had passed we dropped to the ground, and the bush as far as one could see was flattened by that terrible rush.

We found some calves trailing up behind entirely deserted by their mothers; ordinarily this would not have happened. One of them was quite small and did not seen to mind being captured. One of the bulls we fired at we found dead. When skinning him vultures were seen to be sitting on some trees about a hundred yards distant, and on our proceeding to investigate, here was our second bull. Immediately on being hit he had galloped off on his own in a different direction. This is often the procedure when a bull out of a herd is fired at and wounded. He will invariably go off at right angles and is generally not difficult to secure. My friend, who had large experience in animals, was able to tell by the temperature of the fallen beasts whether they had rinderpest or not.

Up in the hills at this place the buffaloes had long thick coats, but in the lower districts, where it was much hotter, their skins were bare and ill-looking. During the rains buffalo move long distances from their ordinary surroundings and at this time are not so much on the alert as in the dry weather.

I used to be under the impression that lions would not kill the largest bulls, preferring buffalo cows. On two occasions I have surprised lions

K

which had recently killed really old bulls, and in each instance noticed the necks of these enormous beasts were broken. Now, it is probably the wonderful knack they have in doing so, yet it seems uncanny to think that a lion weighing 450 lb. can break the neck of an old buffalo bull weighing a ton.

I have often camped near streams where buffalo tracks were numerous, but never have I had one instance of these animals attempting to attack a camp, either by day or night. Should they be walking direct into the sun their vision is poor and they can be approached much more easily. I find this amongst all our animals of usually good vision. The rays of the sun affect that graceful antelope the impala more so than any. Why this should be so I do not know. I have stood and let them walk up to within sixty yards range, which would otherwise be impossible.

In Northern Rhodesia there is usually a big buffalo drive once a year, when the animals are driven for many miles by a large number of natives with assegais, and they are herded into a certain place when many hundreds of warriors attack them at close quarters, killing a large number— incidentally many of the natives also being killed in the terrible encounter. I was indeed sorry that I could not be present at the last big drive and witness the battle of naked men against the brute of beasts—such I describe him on account of the intensity of his vicious fury, premeditated or otherwise.

I would add that these drives are the only methods

which can be employed to keep the animals within bounds. Otherwise they breed to such an extent that the grazing lands of the natives would be entirely used up. Against this we have the outcry against the demolition of the African fauna. Should the animals ever be allowed to multiply to alarming extents, then Nature will adjust herself by the outbreaks of disease, which does not stay there, but finds its uncanny way into the herds of domestic cattle and causes unimaginable loss and expense to the natives themselves and the country concerned, in trying to combat it.

Five years ago I was asked to accompany a filming expedition anxious to get pictures of buffalo herds. The area selected was a regular buffalo stronghold, and in this vicinity I put them at a mean estimate of nearly three thousand. At this time they roamed about on the open plains like cattle. The country was of volcanic origin, actually a continuation of the Great Rift Valley, well known to African travel. This expedition was equipped with several large lorries, and the idea was to have one lorry ahead with the filming apparatus rigged up on a swivel on top of the cab, while another lorry went slowly round from the back, which would drive the buffalo without stampeding them past the ambushed lorry, which was as near the trails as possible and hidden under green foliage.

This drive did not work out as successfully as was expected. Even with the buffalo walking in their own sweet way, great clouds of dust were thrown up by the hoofs of the large number of animals. They gradually came nearer, many hundreds of them, and evidently the driver of the rear lorry was too keen to assist in getting the picture. Immediately he came too near they started running, and as they came nearer the bush where we waited, broke into a gallop. By this time it was impossible to see any buffalo—nothing but a tremendous cloud of dust, more like a sand storm. This cloud came nearer and nearer and very shortly the buffalo simply enfiladed our hidden lorry. They did not see it, and while we were trying to get away from it, a large bull crashed into the lorry, and in his flight actually tried to scramble over the top of the bonnet, his forelegs actually getting on top. This was too close, and he had to be shot away before any damage could be done. We later overcame this difficulty by taking up positions and letting the buffalo walk towards us. In this manner excellent pictures are taken.

Probably the buffalo is the most feared animal of all by the natives. On many occasions I have been hunting elephant or other game and one or more of these beasts has crashed off beside me, the natives having cleared immediately, buffalo and native each going in different directions. One day, without realising it, I walked within a few feet of two buffalo bulls in some thorn bush. I was actually hunting buffalo, and in the shadow of a tree I noticed a solitary old bull. He was fast asleep, as it was about noon, when the day was at its hottest. At fifty yards range I fired and killed him on the ground; he never managed to get up. Going forward to inspect the trophy, imagine my surprise to see two more crash out behind the bush where my dead bull lay. They gave me one glower and tore into space, while I was too surprised to do anything. They usually are so wary, but this is an instance where they never moved when the shot was fired, for not realising their companion was dead gave them confidence to remain. It is the same everywhere you go in Africa; one cannot make a hard and fast rule regarding their habits.

Hunting in one area is somewhat different from another, as they seem to adopt other ways and you have to hunt then accordingly. You shoot two or more in the same place, one seems to take longer to die than the other, such is the extraordinary vitality displayed by some against others. Even though you find some of them die easy, do not underrate him. To sum him up, he is a tough-skinned customer, imbued with indomitable courage and bravery. When wounded he takes to heavy cover; he can be a terrible antagonist and an adversary to be seriously reckoned with. I have shot numbers of these vigorous animals over many years and today I hunt him with even more cunning and cautiousness. Should my remarks assist in saving you from trouble, I shall be amply repaid.

CHAPTER FIFTEEN

Rhino

I WILL now recall to my readers several hunts with that great, lumbering, ungainly beast the rhino. I have seen him at his best and at his worst, and even now I feel I never know what he is going to do next. His one idea at times is to charge anything. Even the unattended Fordson tractor out in the ploughed land has not escaped his attention, so much so that there is an instance of one of these stupid beasts having broken his own neck in trying to kill the iron mass. Not many years ago a certain motorist left his car unattended on a main highway, his petrol having given out, and on returning next day found his car badly damaged. The owner was wroth and returned immediately to the police station, where a report was made against someone for wilful damage. On the police officer arriving, taking notes and inspecting the car, much to the chagrin of the owner the officer took a piece of rhino horn from the radiator; this was stronger evidence than a thumb mark. I cannot see the officer of the law hand-cuffing the culprit !

An amusing incident, though it did not appear so at the time, happened when friends of mine were motoring along the Great North Road between Mpika and Serenji in North-East Rhodesia. When ten miles from Mpika proceeding south, they were surprised to see a rhino cow and calf standing about fifty yards from the narrow highway. Driving very slowly, while his companion was in the act of getting his camera ready to take the picture of these on-lookers, one of them suddenly realised that instead of getting a picture, they would be lucky to evade her oncoming rush. When the car was practically abreast, the rhino put her head down and charged straight at the car, and before the driver realised, the great beast had her horn under the footboard and actually tried to turn the car over. The car weighed two tons and was loaded with one and a half tons of equipment. Notwithstanding this heavy weight, the car was tilted over at a dangerous angle of thirty degrees, when the running board broke off, with portions of the mudguards. The car dropped on the ground. This incident occurred in a few seconds, and the most amusing side of the picture was the rhino going like smoke with its front horn impaled through the eight-foot long board, creating a terrible din, with the broken mudguard hitting on the ground, and the youngster following in her wake squeaking as it ran.

Unfortunately this charge spoiled the prospects of what might have proved an interesting picture, but the artists were indeed fortunate in escaping without injury.

Having shot a number of these beasts, damage doers and otherwise, I have had unique opportunities of exchanging visits with them in camp and out of it. Even today I find him sullen, morose and doubting. In open country he is like the rest of our dangerous game; if he gets a whiff of you he beats it with tail erect, trotting his best, with head constantly half turning to either side. It is in bush forest country that he can be distinctly alarming; he crashes out at no mean speed, puffs and snorts like jets of a steam engine, and more likely than not will run straight into your path. It is here you see him at his worst; his size and the ease with which he gets through the terrible thorn bushes make him all the more formidable.

His sight is dull, but his action is quick in the extreme, and Nature has provided him with death-dealing weapons, in his extremely tough horns. It may interest several to know that these horns are actually composed of fibrous and solidified hairs. Elephants I have found on many occasions give way to rhinos. Twice I have seen them meet, and on each occasion the elephants have seen the rhino first and hustled quickly past while the rhino stood looking, and then moved on without any accelerated speed. This proved to me that the elephant is actually afraid of rhino.

Hunting in elephant country two years ago, I came across a young rhino which was unattended. Natives informed me that the mother had been killed by elephants, as there were many in that place; but, as I had no proof, it was more than likely she fell a victim to their poisoned arrows. I wonder if any of my readers have ever noticed the difference in the blood of the rhino compared with that of any other beast? It adheres to your fingers like gum after exposure to the air for a few minutes. This I found more pronounced with the northern frontier rhinos compared to those in the inland mountains of 6,000 feet, but this may only be attributed to the lesser degree of heat. In many parts today rhinos may be found wandering about in the semi-open bush until nearly noon, especially if it is a cool day accompanied by drizzling rain. He is the easiest animal I know to skin, the thick hide falling off in great folds to the smallest effort of the knife. This can be made into sticks and whips, and is at times useful. I have seen beads, graded down, made from rhino horn, uncommon necklaces of great beauty; there is a sheen, colour and feel about them which is particularly attractive. I am of the opinion that ivory does not compare. When in the Congo North, I saw many figures and ornaments, carved by the natives, made from the horn of the white rhino, and these works, completed with crude tools, certainly gained my admiration.

Many of the oldest bulls are found in quite inaccessible places, their shins lacerated and often suppurating from wounds inflicted by others; and these wounds, heavily infected by flies, mud and slime, take an indefinite time to heal, if ever.

The rhino bird is the friend and enemy of the rhino. In the former case, he will be guided by these birds, which, on approaching danger (up to sixty yards distance), will rise from his back, uttering their harsh " chir chir " notes, when he will wheel round. If they re-alight, he will settle down and stay, otherwise he does not take thought of either sound or smell and hoofs it. Should you see the birds flying overhead in the early morning, and they pass over certain bush, then you know the rhino is not at home; should they fly low and settle, then it is a certainty. This will show that the birds assist both the hunter and the hunted.

Rhinos are still plentiful in Eastern Africa, and horns of thirty inches long are still obtainable, and this measurement may be considered good. When hit I have heard him emit squeals not unlike the domestic pig, and in other ways resemble it. He browses on the shoots of branches and is not averse to the thorn and prickly varieties, his teeth cutting the twigs as if sheared.

The rhino's attack, as a rule, is a direct rush, hoping to impale you in his stride. His massive horns with the ton weight behind are capable of doing great injury. He is not the vicious, cruel type like the buffalo, and I have never heard of a rhino using his feet to stamp you. Even though this morose beast's vision is poor, his sense of hearing and smell are keen, and he is apt to be truculent when you least expect it. I do not consider him difficult to kill, and with a heavy rifle he will swerve off the reports and charge for safety instead of troubling you further.

I will tell an incident against myself. A certain American lady sportswoman, a splendid type, was keen to shoot a rhino. One morning we sallied forth on to some plains intercepted by two streams, and five rhino were seen slowly ambling along. My lady friend was armed with a Remington ·305 calibre rifle, and, as my gun bearer was carrying my spare rifle, a 9·3 Mauser, I suggested that she used this weapon in preference to her Remington. Nothing further was said, and I continued the stalk to the best rhino. At sixty yards range she fired, and that rhino dropped dead, killed with one Peters belted ·225 grained bullet. I had never seen a neater shot, and was expounding on the merits of my 9·3 Mauser when she laughed and said, " But I did not use it." I felt wee ! She had used her own gun. This will show what humane work can be done with accurate shooting from a modern small bore rifle.

That rhino have put the wind up me on many occasions I am quite willing to admit. I recollect having completed a hunt on the Tsavo River and cut across country to a station on the Uganda Railway called Kyulu. Now the distance was roughly fifteen miles, and everything went well for the first seven.

From then onwards I was scouting my way through that painful scrub, " wait-a-bit " thorn bush, and it was difficult enough to find without getting scratched and torn. But to add to the discomfort several rhino charged out in front of me and filled the air with vigorous puffings. I did not think much of this until a mile or so further on, where there was a small valley which held a clear pool of alkaline water. I had barely left this place when I tracked into a regular hornets' nest of rhino. Never have I seen so many; they bolted this way and that, puffing and snorting in the bush. I knew they had not gone but were listening, and it began to tell on my nerves. I am sure I felt my hat lifting many times. My natives fled and I did not blame them. I would have done likewise, but you cannot (at least I admit I cannot) make much headway when you must keep your eyes at the back of your pants as well. I was fast becoming an expert rhino dodger.

At one time I thought of retracing my footsteps, and then I wondered how many of those sullen charging brutes had gone ahead of me. I continued on, and I arrived at the railway line quite three miles below Kyulu station with my clothes a mass of rags, but glad to get away from that accursed spot. I have never been there since and doubt if anyone has, if the native poacher has not found this rhino Mecca. Anyone wanting multiplied thrills will surely find them there.

Apart from being hunted in the day-time I have been routed at night. It was further south, near a place called Fudemayo in Kenya, when, in company with a friend, we were hunting sable antelope. The day had been hot and tiring, and that night I woke up with a thirst. I had only been drinking tea the previous night, and, feeling my way in the dark to the camp table, I felt something soft and fuzzy. Not finding a glass, I lit a lamp, and immediately I did so a trail of driver ants squirmed up my pyjamas and attacked me fiercely. The strange thing is they do not attempt to bite or attack in the dark. They were now getting too hot for me, and I was being bitten without mercy and could stand no more, calling Allen to come to my assistance. Thinking I was in the clutches of a wild

animal, he rushed forward to find me standing, as
Adam, in the garden of Eden, without raiment.
His look was one of astonishment; I am sure he
thought I had gone " loofy." It took his assistance to rid me of the plague. They covered my
bed and clothing, and nothing was safe from them
for some considerable time. A trail of hot ashes
was placed round the camp to get rid of this determined and man-biting string.

That these stupid rhino will " disturb the peace "
I discovered one night when I was camped at the
foot of Ngulia Mountains, Kenya. It was late in
the evening when my safari arrived, and tents were
pitched quickly without noticing that several rhino
trails passed in close proximity, which led to the
stream near by. I might mention that it would
have been difficult to find a suitable place free from
their tracks, which appeared to be everywhere.

That night at about 8 p.m. there were several
snorts and similar noises; one is apt to get used to
them and treat them with diffidence. My porters
had fixed two of their tents (which were made of
white drill cloth). About midnight I heard a
terrible commotion outside, and the heavy gallop
made me at once realise a rhino was in our midst.
Seizing my heavy rifle, I was on the point of rushing
out when I cannoned into a native who was fleeing
into my tent for protection. He was too scared to
make any explanation, and his colour from the usual
black had faded, due to sheer fright. On investigating, I found one of the tents had entirely gone,
carried off on the spikes and head of a rhino,

leaving the natives without injury on the ground. I wonder even now who actually had the worst fright, rhino or natives ! One can imagine a porter's tent transformed into a ghost of the night, and the look of the panic-stricken natives my pen cannot describe.

Next morning we followed the trail of the rhino, and sure enough there were the portions of a perfectly good tent hanging on to the lower branches of " wait-a-bit " thorn bushes which had parted company on his terrible rush. Since that episode I have taken more care in selecting camping sites when in rhino-infested country. I hold several grudges against them. They have not always been kind to me, as my next incident will explain.

Trekking from Kenani station to the Athi River through impenetrable thorn bush was much harder than I had anticipated. I knew that in the dry season there were many big elephants on the Yatta Plateau, which were forced to come down to the river to drink, and my chances of securing heavy ivory were promising. Arranging with twenty natives to carry my kit and stores, we headed into the bush, two natives with slashers in front cutting branches which would facilitate the difficulty of the boys getting my chop boxes through the dense bush.

Within a distance of five miles from Kenani station we encountered rhino, and the noise of the boys cutting disturbed them, but they gave no trouble. Further on I saw a mother rhino and baby; this little one was the size of a collie dog, and

could only have been a few days old. Giving my
porters a rest and not wishing to have any trouble
with an angry cow, I watched the pair for some
time, and it was interesting to see baby suckling
exactly similar to a domestic cow, the mother
standing while it did so.

It seemed strange that they should be so far from
water, at least twelve miles off, but this was possibly
on account of the mother's extra care for her little
charge. Now rhinos, as a general rule, drink once
daily, in the evening, and this little chap, maybe
a week old, was doing his twenty miles a day to the
river and back to the bush they laid up in. This
will give the reader an idea as to the hardy
creatures they are. As we were going to move on,
the natives whistled and yelled at them, and they
made off in the opposite direction.

The making of the way through the bush was a
tiresome process, and it looked as if we would not
reach the Athi River that day, and we did not. In
the afternoon I saw a rhino with a good pair of
horns, and, had it not been for delaying the safari,
would have shot him, but, as we had not prepared
for carrying water, it was out of the question. Fate
willed it otherwise. My safari was keeping well
together in Indian file, and I heard a native shout
" Faro " (this is the Swahili native name for rhino),
and there to our right was an old rhino, big in body,
with one of the most miserable pair of horns I have
seen. He stood about seventy yards off, with ears
extended and head poised in our direction; I could
see the natives casting glances to see if a suitable tree

was near; they evidently did not like the rhino's looks. In a moment he came trotting towards us, rudder straight on end—an ugly-looking customer. Yelling at him, he took no notice, and what was my shout, anyhow? His trot developed into a mad gallop; he charged down on to the line, but, from what I saw, on no one in particular. I knew then what would happen; I heard one chop box crash, then another. My porters were now going helter-skelter, " hell bent for election " speed. I had to shoot this desperate beast, and if only he had owned decent horns it would not have been so bad. Apart from that, here was my disorganised band now thoroughly demoralised. And my outfit! I remember seeing the sack which contained kettles and other camp truck, a bent and derelict lot. Retrieving my flying squad, we had no option but to camp there the night to enable us to take the rhino's hide and horns. Water was the difficulty; we had none, my spare water can had been upset and lost in that mad rush. I sent two natives on ahead to the river, instructing them to return with water for the others, but they did not show up that night, getting bushed on the way.

The heat had been fierce that day coming through that desert bush, and at night I kept my lips moist by making a hole into a tin of Heinz baked beans and sucking it. When morning came I was indeed pleased, and we started off, meeting the two boys on the way whom we had sent to the river the previous night. Arriving at the river was a welcome sight after the trials of the previous day.

That afternoon I went along the river bank up-stream to see what the possibilities were; there was plenty of spoor of elephants, buffalo and rhino drinking here. It was indeed interesting to sit on the bank of this shallow river and see rhinos coming down to drink in the late afternoon. Between 5.30 and 6 p.m. I counted nine of them drinking in a stretch of half a mile. It was evident they had never been disturbed here previously by white men, and here Nature was at her best. The distance from the river to the foot-hills of a steep escarpment was about four miles. I wonder how many hundreds of rhino were living in that area at this dry time of the year. I should say many, such are the numbers of these animals in Kenya Colony today.

Returning to my quest, the elephants. From 8 p.m. that night until midnight you could hear the animals splashing and gurgling in the river as they bathed and drank, notes varying from the high-pitched scream of the cow elephants to the deep outbursts of the bulls. It would be difficult to estimate how many of these big bulls watered there regularly while the drought lasted. I have scouted round the foot-hills adjoining and seen wide and deep tracks worn out and down by elephants' feet during the past centuries. There they have a stronghold and there they will remain for centuries to come, the country here being quite uninhabited, and apart from the native poachers has seldom been hunted by man, and the district lends itself to no other use than holding game.

L

Apart from the river it is an uninteresting place—no water, and desert thorn in abundance. The bush appears dry and sapless, but immediately after a little rain the whole country appears green, an unbelievable transformation, such is the forced and rapid growth. Natives seeking honey (who are in reality camouflaged poachers, their bows and arrows hidden in the surrounding bush) came into my camp, and immediately wanted to take me to the elephants. I agreed to go out next morning and see what we could find; these natives, I found, knew every track, in fact every trail in that little-known district. They would skirt a particular stretch of bush because rhino were there, and their idea, which was a sound one, was to stay the night on top of rocky kopjes in the valley and watch from the summit to see the biggest bulls passing to and from the river. I found method in their ways, and my hunt proved most successful.

These natives are great meat eaters, and a few years ago when a bonus of so much per pound was paid on ivory " found " and brought into a station, these natives harvested well. This was entirely as they wished it, as they would shoot many elephants with their poisoned arrows, eat the meat, bury the tusks, and after a lapse of three months unearth the ivory, bring it into a Government Boma and claim their reward, setting the onus against some European for having wounded one, or more, elephant and then lost it. The Game Department, now alive to this form of poaching, put an end to a vicious practice. The result is that today more elephants live, as the native would not think of killing unless he could make profit from it. Lions in these out-lying places are never molested by natives for the sport or fun of it, but if you put a price on the hides they will come along, such is the brain of our native poaching fraternity. On this I will say more anon.

Up to date I have actually only come across one rhino wounded by the natives' arrow. I was traversing an area in the Sonsa country border-ing between Kenya and Tanganyika, and spotting a big rhino bull, I could not understand why he was so uneasy; he kept stamping round in a circle and appeared to be in pain. Moving in his direction, I could see an arrow sticking in his side, the steel or iron part next the point being bent over. Going nearer him—some rhino birds flew off his back—he came in my direction in a determined charge of blind fury. I shot him and then examined the arrow wound; this had passed between his ribs, the iron stem of the arrow being polished on account of the rhino rubbing it against trees to dislodge it. The poison substance had entirely disappeared, and it is most probable that this had been old and baked, losing its paralysing properties.

Some years ago a tragedy under distressing cir-cumstances occurred to one of two sportsmen, father and son, who proceeded to hunt rhinos. They hunted for several days, and luck had been invariably against them. One morning, seeing a good bull, they carefully reached within shot and killed him. While looking at him lying dead a second rhino from thick bush adjoining charged out with unprovoked aggression and, before they realised it, knocked the father down, the horn inflicting terrible injuries. The son shot the rhino and then had to proceed a distance of eighteen miles for medical aid. When he arrived his feet were bleeding and lacerated, having run most of the way over terrible stony ground. When they returned to the scene of the tragedy his father had died from the effect of his terrible injuries. This will show that an accident like the above will happen very easily.

A Dutch hunter friend of mine, a man of the bush and one of the best hunters I have ever known, met with a similar accident, the muscles of his thigh being lacerated by the onrush of one of these dangerous beasts. He was taken unawares and entirely off his guard, his lasting regret that he did not get time to put an end to the rhino's senseless fury. The same might have happened to myself. One afternoon I was sitting near a belt of bush, smoking my pipe of peace, and my rifle was some little distance away from me. When I happened to glance behind there was an enormous rhino bull walking straight on to me. He seemed to come from nowhere, and yet with all his bulk and weight I never heard him. I made a grab for my rifle, and none too soon. Had I been without one I must have been at his mercy, as there was no protection near me. Since then I have always made a fixed rule of having my life protector near me. I will conclude my rhino escapades with a brush-up a party and myself had in taking a female rhino's picture, of which she entirely disapproved.

We had hunted all morning for a suitable rhino subject. During the forenoon we had seen several rhinos, the trouble being that they were standing under thorn trees, and from the picture point of view unattractive. The outlook was not very hopeful until someone spotted a rhino by an isolated tree. She was standing about 200 yards away and not marred by heavy undergrowth or long grass, and everything pointed to a successful picture. We walked up towards her, and as we came nearer discovered there were two rhinos. Evidently one had been lying down, which was now standing beside the one we had previously seen. The idea was to get up to them as close as possible without their detecting our presence. Everything was working splendidly, the wind, though little, in our favour, and the light good. At sixty yards a standard 35 mm. cine was rigged up and filming commenced. It was now easy to discern the sex, a cow and her offspring; there was little difference in their size. The idea of approaching a little closer was suggested and acted upon. Slowly and cautiously we sneaked up to within twenty-five yards and were not detected. The cine on its tripod was fixed up, and at the first noise of the release, the cow promptly turned to the sound, ears all alert, to catch the direction of the strange noise. Finding this, she took a few steps forward, and now the situation did not look so good. My friend the operator—I give him full marks—kept on that starter

and the next instant she charged straight on to us.
I do not know what fraction of a second she took to
cover the intervening yards; it must have been little.
I saw the film later. She received two shots and
crashed only six feet from the tripod, a cloud of
dust, as she struck the ground on her massive snout,
flying all round us. When the charge came home,
I noticed the young one was at her right side and
slightly behind from the time she did that terrible
rush. The surprising thing was that no one saw the
young one go, as the dust the mother raised on
falling obscured it.

That even the sound of a cine motor is strange
to all animals, and is readily picked up, means that
photography on foot is not an easy thing and,
without protection, is, to put it mildly, dangerous.
Even so, with all their bad qualities and their good
horns, the rhino will still remain one of our sporting
beasts worthy of being hunted and entitled to all
the respect given to those animals classified under
the heading " Dangerous."

Hippo

THE hide of the river horse of Africa is thicker than that of the rhino, but when made into sticks is affected by damp weather and does not retain its shape compared to the latter. Here we have an unwieldy beast weighing when fully matured nearly three tons. He is to be found in the majority of the lakes and rivers in Eastern, Southern and Central Africa. There they are in very large numbers, and from the hunting point of view uninteresting. He can boast of the largest mouth of any animal in Africa, and has used it on many occasions on mankind with fatal results. That the hippo can be most ferocious—more especially if it is an old, war-scarred, bad-tempered bull, when he will attack canoes, actually biting them in half, including the occupants—is only too well known.

On Lake Victoria there has been from time to time considerable loss of life, and this form of hunting, unless you are a good swimmer, can be decidedly dangerous. Hippo flesh is eagerly sought by the natives, and the fat is amongst the best known and ideal for European cooking. I have eaten excellent biltong made from the flesh near the ribs, and the flavour always reminds me of the Cockney selling rabbits in London: " Who'll buy the rabbits with the porky flavour ?" The hippo has the latter.

He is a most powerful swimmer, as his name would imply, and, like all other aquatic animals which take to the water head first, he submerges rearwards and can remain under for ten minutes if necessary. They emit peculiar short grunts, and in fact, I doubt if the English dictionary has the words to fit the sound. He is a shapeless mass with the exception of a graceful curve over the shoulder and neck, if it can be so termed. His only defence are his tremendous jaws, which are more than formidable. I have actually seen great chunks taken from the sides of a heavy boat, with as much ease as if it had been matchwood, by these hard biting brutes.

Crocodiles usually inhabit the lakes and rivers in which they are found, but I have never known crocodiles to attack them except when they are dead. Then these avaricious creatures, that seem to know immediately the hippo is helpless, will tear at their head and feet. Hippo will use the same paths leading from pools for years, many of these being worn down (on the lower Mara River) to a depth of four feet. It is also interesting to see the double path made, their feet in one track making a distinct ridge or camber in the centre. When they are not disturbed they will leave the water after dark, proceeding to the open country for a distance of two miles or more, and then they will graze throughout the night, returning to the stream at 5 a.m.

In the water they do not as a rule offer a large target, coming to the surface and bobbing down again, making the brain shot uncertain. The telescopic rifle sight overcomes the difficulty and also minimises the risk of wounding animals, which is much in its favour. When shot in the brain they sink and usually come to the surface in one hour, the gases formed making buoyant their three-ton carcase. When shot in the shoulder, as a rule they will turn over and over, making a heavy splashing noise in the water. In this manner they rapidly drown, when the same procedure will apply. As hippo are more or less heavy feeders the gases rise very quickly, and I have seen many carcases come to the surface within forty minutes of being killed. If pursued while on land and run to their refuge in the river they will not hesitate to take perpendicular banks, even up to fifteen feet deep; the enormous bulk on striking the water can be heard several hundred yards away.

On Lakes Victoria and Albert they are most numerous, although up to a few years ago they were heavily shot on the western side of the latter, which belongs to the Congo Belge. On the Victoria Nile, up to the Murchison Falls in Uganda, there are a considerable number of them which disport themselves to the amusement of sightseers who go up on recognised tours. I am of the opinion they are uninteresting animals compared to lions or other fauna, and in Nature's best handiwork these sluggish " three-ton babies " were ill-favoured.

I have accompanied many expeditions taking African game pictures. Amongst these was an enthusiast who was keen on getting a close-up

picture of these animals as they made the water
break or boil coming to the surface, similar to the
boil of a fish, but on grander scale. We had two
boats attached to our tug, one of them a heavy,
flat-bottomed, steel type and the other a light
wooden one. My friend was keen on taking out
the latter, as it would be more easily handled. Now,
I funked the idea and advocated against this, as
I have seen frail, narrow-bottomed craft upset
before. We decided on the heavy steel one.

Spotting a big herd of thirty of these " bulky
hulks," we rowed amongst them. They sank
immediately and we soon began to get all the
" boils " and " breaks " we wanted. One big
bull pushed his enormous head up within a few
feet of us and I saw his evil eyes. His intent was
bad. In the next few minutes our flat-bottomed
boat shook and keeled partly over with one of the
broad backs of these beasts which tried to upset
it, and I saw part of him as he plunged away
to the right. My enthusiast now lost all interest
in photographs and we rowed away as quickly as
possible, my friend remarking, " Hunter, I guess
you were right." Had we taken out the small
wooden boat there is not the foggiest but that we
would have been upset and have taken our last
picture in Uganda.

I accompanied a Yale University student on a
big game hunt not many years ago, and although
he had a lot of excitement amongst other animals,
a large hippo bull gave him the greatest thrill of
all. Camping near a deep pool on one of our

largest rivers, we were out and away beyond the
pale and ken of the ordinary hunting routes. Here
we were in wild yet wonderful country, game
everywhere, and the music and howls of the denizens
at night made it all the more interesting. The
river here was very beautiful; on the opposite bank
were tall graceful palm trees and bird life, of
brilliant plumage, abundant. There were many
large rocks in the centre of the river, on which
greater and lesser kingfishers settled to gorge their
catches.

Hunting on his birthday had been singularly
lucky, as this bright fellow from Yale shot two
fine maned lions, and, while shooting them over
again at supper, we heard quite close to the camp
the grunt, grunt of a hippo. Now hippos are
prone to be attracted by a light, and we did not
want this mud horse's company, so agreed to shoot
him, if he was worth while, Jerry taking a heavy
double rifle, while I took a torch, as it was quite
dark and the heavy bush adjoining on the river
bank added to its blackness. There were several
old disused hippo trails or roads leading down to
the water fifty yards distant, and we walked down
one of these, trusting we would not meet the great
weighty beast on the way. Arrived at the pool,
I shone the light to the centre towards some rocks
and spotted the eyes of a crocodile. My friend
Jerry evidently saw some other movement between
the rocks and where we stood, and flashing my
light, imagine my horror when in front of us at
a distance of ten feet appeared the head of an

enormous hippo. He did not keep us waiting; he charged forward, whether at the light or me or both of us, I troubled not, as I saw that tremendous mouth wide open; it was hardly possible to believe its expansion. It looked all mouth and spikes. That hippo was quick; Jerry was likewise, and I can see those great jaws close as my friend shot into the centre. He had swallowed his last pill. We did not wait longer, but returned to the camp and hoped to find him in the morning. Of one thing we were certain: we had stopped his grunt and were eager for morning to come to see what sort of teeth this old chap held.

During the night the harsh cough of a leopard was heard near the camp, and as we had a bait near by our chances looked promising for the morning. We were early astir before daybreak and went cautiously over to the tree which held our bait. When at a distance of seventy yards, there was the head of a very big leopard peering past the side of it and staring at us. It was a difficult shot, and my friend, throwing up his rifle, fired, and just as he pulled that trigger so did the leopard pull back his head, the bullet hitting the place it had been a bare fraction previously. At the report he streaked across to the nearest bush in several tremendous long springs and was lost, one of the bullets just grazing him as he fled, which he acknowledged with a low grunt and a flick of his tail. We trailed him for some distance, but it was quite impossible to come up with him; meanwhile hunting boys from our camp came running to inform us they had seen the dead hippo in the water anchored against a large rock in the centre of the river. Returning to camp and breakfasting, we arranged ropes which could be utilised for dragging him to the river bank. Arriving, there was the hippo, purple-stained belly through discolouration by blood, having been dead all night and his legs sticking up. A large crocodile slid into the water from an adjacent rock and you could see his evil, cunning eyes showing above the water near where he had entered.

Now, until this crocodile showed himself several of the natives were clamouring to swim out and tether the rope on to one of the hippo's legs, but now not one of them would tackle it. With the noise of the natives the crocodile disappeared from view, but doubtless he was in close proximity. In the meantime I saw the bold Yale student taking off his khaki shooting jumper and boots. I asked him what he intended doing; he promptly replied, " Going in." Now here was a brave deed turned down by all the African porters, and I did admire his sporting spirit, even more so after what transpired at his first plunge. The water in the stream was cloudy and it was quite impossible to guess the depth. I arranged to fire two shots into the water near the place where the large crocodile was last seen, while Jerry tied the end of a length of thin cord on to his waist, which would be utilised for hauling the stout rope to attach to the hippo. The embankment over the river bank was about six feet high where I saw Jerry standing preparatory to diving. As there were lots of jagged rocks in the stream bed and the colour of the water obscured them, I suggested to Jerry it would be safer to wade in lest he fouled some of these dangerous pieces. Not he; he took the plunge and I saw him disappear, a perfect dive. Now what happened? He seemed a long time in showing to the surface and when he did I saw his head come slowly up, bleeding badly, with the water running from his wavy hair. I saw a deep lacerated wound caused by having hit one of these hidden perils of the river. He was dazed and it was with some difficulty that I dragged him up on to the embankment. Several of the natives in the meantime bolted, thinking he had been bitten by one of these skulking monsters. Many natives in Africa, especially in the backwoods, are prone to this. A European hunter gets killed or mauled and they will make themselves scarce and not touch the victim, thinking they will be implicated or blamed for the tragedy. After a few minutes Jerry recovered himself and, not dismayed, insisted on another try, while he was in this mood. He was a stout fellow and it is a credit to that great overseas university to turn out fellows such as he. This time he did not dive, but waded in from the trail of a hippo and swam out to the already ballooned beast which did not add to the beauty of the river. Pulling the rope to him only occupied a few minutes, and this was hitched round the hind leg, when, with the aid of all the natives in camp, the expanded carcase was soon hauled to the bank.

This old bull must have roamed in that stream for many years; his hide was heavily scratched and scored with trade marks of the other bulls' teeth in their many squabbles, either for possession of the pool or the opposite sex. Taking off his head and skin was difficult, as this had to be done in three feet of water, where he was stranded. Leaving the carcase as a bait for crocodile, we secured several of these voracious beasts, and I am confident that had Jerry known that such numbers existed in that stream, he would have shot his hippo elsewhere. I would !

Camping near Ziwani swamp four years ago, overlooked by Afric's grandest snow-clad mountain, Kilimanjaro, we were doing a general hunt. Here there were masses of game from elephant to the smallest antelopes. It was quite hot here in the daytime, but the sight of the snow on the massive peaks seemed to cool the air. During full moon I have sat and viewed this wondrous spectacle in Africa's midst, and listened to the lion's roar on the foot-hills adjoining. Surely a wondrous sight which would thrill the heart of anyone and inspire the poet's mind. This place was the commencement of the Tsavo River, immortalised in that book " The Man Eaters of Tsavo."

The river in some places is only six feet wide and is a series of deep pools, mud fish, barbel and eels being plentiful, which the boys from camp took a delight in catching.

One morning two of our natives came running from the camp stating that an enormous " kiboko "

(Swahili word for hippo) had tried to eat them in the stream below. Now one of the natives was a lazy one—I had never seen him put his best foot forward, like this effort; this made me feel there must be an essence of truth in it. Taking our rifles, we went to investigate, and there were the boys' fishing bait and their pants left beside a narrow part of the stream. Now to dislodge the hippo. A brain wave presented itself. A large pole was cut, the idea being to probe it into the pool while another watched with a rifle. The first pool proved a blank, but at the tail end of the next my pole friend evidently gave this old bull hippo a dig in the ribs, and that hippo, thoroughly infuriated, gave a tremendous bound forward, grunting in the act, and tried to scramble up the low embankment, mouth wide open and eyes a mass of fury. The report of a rifle rang out, the bullet hitting him near the ear and the mass slid back on his hindquarters into the stream, deader than mutton. I wondered why the hippo had taken to this small stream, but discovered that natives had been burning the reeds (their cover) in Ziwani swamp, which had caused the old chap to leave and run into the jaws of " man the destroyer."

An incident with alarming results happened when an American tourist found himself at Livingstone in Northern Rhodesia, and expressed his keen desire to obtain cine pictures of hippos in their breeding grounds, which are near the junction of the Chobi River and the Zambesi. There is quite an island formed there, and the backwaters are the well-known breeding grounds for hippos. Now no native will take his canoe into this place, but a few natives yielded to a tempting sum and agreed to take their canoe into the dreaded waters. Everything went well until the canoe gained an entrance, when immediately a female hippo made a dash for the canoe, nearly upsetting it. This was evidently the beginning, for more of these bulky monsters took the offensive, another of them taking the bow of the canoe in her great mouth, squashing it as though it were a match-box. The canoe sank immediately, the American tourist and one native just managing to swim ashore, while one of the natives was killed in the attempt for safety. Needless to relate, the whole cine apparatus found a resting-place on the floor of the hippos' pool and a disgruntled visitor, sadder, but wiser, appreciated the car lift back to Livingstone. It is little, or big, arguments like this which make these beasts worthy of their photos being taken.

M

Leopard

FROM the clumsy to the alert, agile and dangerous animal, the leopard, we have a fearless and savage foe. These animals are widely distributed over most of Africa, and many of their skins are very beautiful, especially the heavily dark spotted variety, which is met with in the forests and surrounding hills. The fact that leopard skin coats have added to the grace and charm of many women is responsible for the fact that these beasts have been hunted a great deal, irrespective of the dangers accompanying the pursuit. I often wonder how many tussles were encountered before the certain matchings of a specific coat were completed, as the select pieces are only chosen in doing so. The black leopard is found in Abyssinia, and I have also seen the same melanistic variety in the southern Congo Belge, the dull markings or spots showing distinctly in certain lights and angles. They are certainly beautiful skins, but in my opinion cannot be compared with the magnificent pelts of the snow leopard from the Himalayas.

Hearing some guinea fowl call in the undergrowth while in the Congo, I ventured forth with a scatter gun, and on approaching them a fine black leopard jumped up a few feet from me, snarled, and made into the high grass and was lost to view immediately. I was too surprised to do anything, and number six shot in his hide would probably have been to his gain and my detriment. Natives from this post informed me that there were many of them, which was apparent from the worn skins they adorned themselves with. Evidently this black beauty and myself both had covetous eyes on the same flock of birds.

That I have seen and killed a great number of leopards there can be no disputing, both with rifle shot and trap gun, and believe me, kill him any way you can, he will assuredly meet you on the same terms, expecting no more and giving no less. Their movements are invariably quicker than your eye, and if you follow him wounded into cover the chances are against you, even if you are armed with the most efficient death-dealing piece known.

He is imbued with a savage cunning, will hold his spring until he is practically certain of his range, usually five yards, when he will spring for your head and eyes and, if lucky, commence on you with all four paws and teeth at the same time, the very essence of temper and attack lust. His fury is second to none, and blood poisoning is apt to result from his poisonous claws. He is a filthy feeder, preferring his food in a decomposed stage.

During the rainy season he is difficult to see on account of the long grass, only his harsh, deep, coughing voice, somewhat like the noise of two cross-cut saws in unison, letting you know of his presence. It is when the grass is burnt down in the dry season that he is not difficult to secure, and in the uninhabited parts I have not found him any more difficult to bag than lion. He will allow an automobile to approach him up to sixty yards, and like the lion does not couple it with an enemy. In the next fifty years it will be interesting to note if the animals are born with a different temperament and will realise that motor-cars are the components of their dreaded foe—mankind. They are the wariest of all our animals and usually have their cubs, three in number, amongst rocks, the large hollows in trees or in the cellars of ant bear burrows. Wart hogs, bush buck, and the smaller antelopes are their principal food in the distant wilds, but near habitation the domestic dog is their great attraction, to which subject I shall refer later.

There are remote instances where they have been accused as man eaters and as such would be more feared than their bigger kin, the lion, on account of their more daring and desperate cunning. This type take to killing calves, and I had the pleasure of exterminating one such pest, a riddance of Africa's worst. At times they will charge with lightning rapidity, and lucky is he who can then fire from the hip or otherwise, as the probability is you would not get time to raise the rifle to your shoulder. It is here that the 12 bore shotgun loaded with heavy shot, 3A or SS9, can prove the " bushman's friend " when in the way of that vicious spring, charged to the hilt with cruelty. He has the knack of being able to hide in the smallest cover, and your surprise is afterwards as to how he was able to do it. I have never seen one attempt to charge in an open plain, but then this applies to all African fauna. Under cover of darkness Nature has imbued him with savage daring, for he will approach a dead bait without fear; after allowing him to feed for several minutes I have switched a torch on him, when he has stopped for a minute or so and then continued feeding under its glare. This naturally would be governed by the intensity of his hunger.

Leopards are excellent climbers, being able to negotiate any smooth climbs by the dexterous use of their claws, fore and aft. I have never heard of anyone being attacked in Africa by these vicious creatures when waiting over a kill; but in Rhodesia natives have informed me that lions, the man-eating type, have been known to and will climb up a tree, and, maybe out of curiosity, inspect any such hide or machan, before settling down to feed on the carcase or bait underneath. It is feasible that these lions, having been hunted for the past century, have now been born with a more cunning temperament than formerly and, alive to the possibility of their final extinction, have acquired this safer habit, and are a long way ahead, in wisdom, of our East African species.

Three years ago when hunting with a large party of foreign sportsmen in Kenya, eight leopards were accounted for in one month's hunting, and all shot in the open sitting near ravines in the early morning and late afternoons. It is only when near civilisation that they will retreat into cover of heavy bush, only venturing out under cover of darkness. Where guinea fowls frequent, and come down to drink in the late evenings, is an excellent place to visit and find these wary creatures, sitting in dry sandy rivers and all intent on the bird. Frequently I have shot leopards in this manner by peering over the embankments, getting easy shots.

The incident I am now going to relate will give my readers an insight into the great daring displayed at times by these savage animals. I accompanied in my professional capacity a newly married army officer and his wife—a charming couple. His wife had a splendid specimen of Alsatian dog to which she was much attached. We had been hunting on the western side of Kenya and the safari a big success. One time of this interesting hunt found our party on the ridge of a prominent plateau overlooking the vast, little-known plains in the distance below. This couple—I will now call them my friends—had a first-class double fly tent, complete with verandah, under which we usually dined. When they retired for the night, their faithful Alsatian usually slept on the floor near the lady's bed. One night at about 10 p.m. there was a terrible commotion inside, and when a torch was flashed there was a large leopard in their tent, and it was in a desperate struggle with the dog. The leopard, seeing it was detected, bolted through the door of their abode and disappeared under darkness. It was then found that the leopard had cautiously sneaked into the tent, without even arousing this wonderful watchdog's attention, and further examination showed that the leopard gripped the dog by the back of the neck, but was foiled in the act of killing it by a prominent brass stud—fastened on to the collar—hindering the top jaw from driving in its terrible fangs. Next day a gun-trap was arranged near their camp and that leopard paid the price for his daring, and on examination there was the abrasion in the roof of the leopard's mouth caused by the pyramid stud on the dog's collar.

Now this will give you an idea of what hope or chance mankind could have of detecting the presence of such animals at night.

When hunting elephants in the Makindu area, a native came along to me to shoot a leopard which he informed me was caught in a steel trap. I agreed to do so and in the distance heard the continual yelping of a dog. Approaching I now found that this native had his dog in a box as bait, and a steel trap similar to those used for trapping foxes had been set at the edge of the box into which the leopard had trodden. I also saw why the native had come for my assistance. He had fired an arrow into this infuriated beast, the wooden shaft being plainly visible sticking in its hind-quarters. This leopard when approached was the picture of living fury. It growled, snarled and spat all seemingly in one breath, and when I was within forty yards charged in one terrific spring. The trap on its hind toes seemed to make little hindrance. I hit it with my first shot, but it was not good enough, and my next just spoiled the look of that skin, much to the native's disgust, who spat on the ground with contempt for my bad shooting, as I had shot its head practically off. This was typical of natives' gratitude, as skins at the time were selling at £4 each. When I examined this leopard, I found the trap had just gripped the toes, and in a comparatively short time he would have freed himself by leaving these mementoes behind. That it was a terrible ordeal for the dog was without question, but the value of the skin came before the dog, which is typical of these gentlemen.

Why leopards should prefer the flesh of dogs I do not know. The dog, irrespective of size, is to them a favourite meal. Leopards depend entirely on their caution and the onset of their sudden attack, the dog being held in the fast death grip and unable to make any resistance. Even their contempt for my own home was proved by a crackling of bones on the verandah one night about 9 p.m., and on switching on the electric light I was surprised to see one of these prowling cats on the verandah. He had been eating chicken bones left from the dinner table. On my approach he bolted, and luckily for him he did not return.

CHAPTER EIGHTEEN

A Terror of the Night

WHEN employed shooting lions, which were doing a considerable amount of damage to stock, I had an urgent message from some elderly Masai chiefs to assist them in ridding their locality of an enormous leopard which had killed several calves in their kraal, and was the terror of this pastoral people. Visiting this place next day, I had pointed out to me their latest loss, a young heifer bitten through the throat, and I immediately made my plans to sit up for that killing marauder the same night.

The country near the kraal was ideal leopard country, rocky, interspersed with thorn bush. It would have been quite useless to attempt to hunt this part with any degree of success, and I was fully confident of bringing the pest to book under cover of darkness. Finding a suitable bush near the scene of his last victim, I hollowed it out and arranged to wait that night, the Masai when I entered it giving me their quaint blessings. I was hopeful of this terror returning early in the night, but it did not materialise. At about 3 a.m., when I had had a long night vigil, I saw the outline of an animal coming forward in the dimness of the clear starry night. It looked to me too big for an ordinary leopard and most like the shape of a lioness. I would mention that beasts at night appear much larger to the human eye than they really are and can be deceptive. I watched this animal come forward, sneaking and not making a sound. One's eyes get used to picking up objects at night after practice which to the ordinary on-looker would be invisible; this is my opinion for what it is worth. I speak solely from experience, being able to discern objects which to the ordinary layman would not be spotted. It is always an awesome feeling waiting and watching at night, and when my thoughts have fled back to a comfy bed, you wonder, at least I have, why I do these things. I had made up my mind as soon as this beast came within fifteen yards to give him or her a bullet. I did not have long to wait before seeing that crouch-ing outline, deciding to shoot low on him, as it was quite impossible to see my front sight, and the danger when shooting at night is to over shoot. I poked my rifle through the bush and fired. At the report I heard a muffled grunt and the noise of his bound as he darted into the thicket on my right. I did not hear the thud of the bullet, but then at close range you seldom do, and my thoughts went riot. Had I missed ? I felt now I should have waited longer, but I was so tired of waiting that my nerves, if I have any, were all taut and overstrung and I just had to fire. At the report of my rifle the cattle and donkeys in the kraal nearby started a terrible din, and I could hear the voices of natives inside, but no one ventured out, and I would have acted likewise. They expected, I am confident, to see their danger dead, and he was not. I listened, but in vain, to hear any sounds of dying groans nearby.

Next morning at dawn I examined the spot where the leopard had been standing when I fired. There were the unmistakable marks of his claws dug into the bare earth as he tried for leverage in his spring for safety. I followed in; here was blood; my thoughts ran high. I would follow until we met. As soon as it was light enough to see the Masai came out of their huts, which are actually made of plastered cattle dung, and all around long polished spears. Following the trail he led towards a small ravine and had lain down; the colour of the blood being light red showed me there was a big possibility of his being alive and able to resist. He was, from the spoor, walking and had the use of his legs, so it was evident I had missed his shoulder.

Within a hundred yards one of the Masai had a glimpse of him stealing towards a bush twenty yards to the right of the trail we were following. To avoid him springing at us from the flank, we left the trail and went direct towards the bush. I knew we would have trouble, and wishing to avoid anyone getting mauled I fired at a dark movement in the centre, reloading immediately. At once he responded with a snarl and came out charging at the lot of us, no one in particular. His forearm was broken by my first shot. This considerably hindered his speed and he fell an easy victim. When secured, the whole of that kraal, men, women and children, began dancing round the carcase, the younger men being restrained with difficulty from ruining the skin with their spears.

This was an exceptionally big leopard of the forest type, beautifully marked and measuring eight feet long before skinning. I found, as I surmised, that my bullet from the previous night had gone too high and passed through his body without breaking any important bones. My keenness had overcome my aim. It is really surprising how over-excitement and keenness can affect the tyro in his initiative hunts in the African bush. I suppose it is the same with all, not excepting myself. Excitement seems to get the better of your aim, the point of the rifle seems to wobble and is inclined to make circles. The three-hundred-yard sight is used when the range is about sixty and you wonder why you shot high. Discovering your error, you get bothered and hot, hoping to improve, and the whole outfit seems wrong; you cannot hit what you fire at. You even question the notch in the back sight. Would it be better to alter the U into a V, but in any case what other word in the alphabet would have made any difference to this day's sticky effort?

The strain of waiting for any animal to get up, maybe a lion or a dik-dik or a covey of partridges, in rising makes your very heart-beat even faster. You make mistakes you have never done before or dreamt possible, jerking your trigger instead of squeezing it, and take solace firing your rifle at a target in camp to correct your errors encountered that day. On your next effort you become a saner man, taking it easy, and you now select the one animal and get him, instead of centring on the herd as yesterday and getting nothing. It is surprising how a bullet under these circumstances will find its way past a herd to delve into mother earth.

I am afraid I am shooting off the mark now, and will return to a leopard hunt in which I witnessed two natives getting mauled within a few feet of me, the time taken to do so being truly unbelievable. The leopard's action was of lightning rapidity in which he literally flew from one to the other and was blown off him at muzzle range, but not before severe injuries had been inflicted.

I was shooting up lions which were doing damage amongst native cattle when a Masai warrior informed me that a party of his tribe had seen a leopard running up a ravine and would assist me in its destruction. I was only too pleased to accompany him to the place they had last seen the animal; the hunt commenced. Meeting some more of this clan, we followed the leopard, the Masai sticking their spears into any bush likely to conceal him. After hunting for some distance one of these warriors spotted him and the rest of them all sprinted after him, yelling as they ran. The leopard, finding the chase and noise too much for his liking, made for some large rocks and took refuge in a cave. One of the natives peered in where he had entered, but not a sign or murmur was seen or heard. Two of the braves then thought they could dislodge him by using a long pole and pushing it up in his direction. This was forthcoming after some difficulty, as straight poles are not easily found in that sandy, unfertile country. These natives were now going to use their double-bladed swords, which are made out of imported single-edged Brades Pangas, while I would stand by with my rifle. They were all excitement as this knotted stick was pushed up the entrance, quivering as they stood. The leopard was obliging, and he came out of that entrance as quickly as a rabbit would bolt to a ferret: you could hear the rattling as he came along and charged straight at the nearest Masai, who never managed to get his sword down from the raised hitting position. The leopard seemed to jump from one to the other, a squirming and terribly enraged beast, his eyes one mass of livid fury. I pushed my rifle against his neck, pulled the trigger, and I saw his jaws release and his tail straighten from that vicious curl as he fell. The natives were plucky and brave, but from what I saw even half a dozen were no match for him in a hand-to-hand encounter. Being too close to him made it more or less impossible to use their slashing knives. When the Liwaru Keri (Masai name for leopard) was dead, in their frenzy they slashed it to pieces with their knives, blaspheming it with oaths as they did so.

The two natives were both scratched and bitten on the front of their thighs and the right arms. These were treated with B.I.P. within a few minutes, but even so the wounds swelled up and caused them severe pain which was accompanied by high fever. This continued for the following two days, after which time they gradually recovered from their short and snappy mauling.

I have seen many leopards shot during the night-time and have never followed a wounded one under these circumstances as I consider it suicidal to do so, as the skin and responsibility of your bearers or yourself is of more importance than the skin of the leopard, be it either black or spotted. Having killed a great number of them, I give him full marks for his great determination and cunning cruelty. To hunt him, if wounded, in cover is a distinctly unhealthy pastime, which if persisted in will end in disaster to the hunter, the chances not being even, and I have no hesitation in placing the odds at six to four with the leopard.

In giving these remarks I have not done so with a view to intimidating the hunter, but with a view to saving him from getting scratched unnecessarily. One's own judgment will be able to tell one just how badly he is wounded or handicapped by the wound inflicted. The chief danger is in an animal shot in the stomach which has the full use of his legs, which enables him to make those " quicker than the eye can follow " charges.

Living in the same veldt we invariably find the cheetah or hunting leopard. Here is an animal who, although often confused with the former, does not have the same vicious habits or temper. They are common on the vast plains where thousands of the smaller gazelles roam, and are usually met with in groups of from three to five. The cubs make ideal pets, and many of these animals are sent to

India from this continent, where they are used for
hunting purposes.   They are, even when wounded,
not dangerous to approach, confining themselves to
snarling and growling and spitting, and in all my
varied experiences I have not seen one actually
charge.

I found in Rhodesia that these animals come
under the heading of vermin, and this is probably
due to the fact that they kill sheep and goats, but
in places where game is plentiful they confine their
attentions to the latter, and do not kill stock in the
East African areas.   He is considered to be the
fastest animal in the world, and I have watched him
kill Grant's and Thomson's gazelles, simply flying
over the surface with a long swinging gallop.   He
climbs remarkably well, notwithstanding the fact
that his claws are similar to those of a dog.

In parts of Kenya and Tanganyika I have seen
as many as a dozen of these nice and harmless
creatures in one day's hunting.   Their skin, compared to that of the leopard, is a poor trophy, and
it seems a pity in many ways that these fleet grey-
hounds of the African veldt should be molested
beyond the pale of civilisation.   They are interesting and do not kill wantonly; their usual poise,
peering over the flat-topped ant-hills on our veldt,
would be missed.   They prefer to kill their own
game, and are clean feeders compared to the lion
or leopard.   I have had cubs of both the ordinary
and hunting species, the former taking the keenest
delight in gorging out of all proportion and pulling
the inside out of any cushion he could get his teeth

into, whereas the latter would be more of a companion and show his appreciation in purring, against the growling of the other. Likable creatures.

Living and killing on the same ground are packs of wild dogs, as a rule mangy and ravenous scourges, who mangle and destroy, and woe unto the animal selected by one of these fleet-footed packs. Their staying power is uncanny, and the sight of their victim, usually torn and mangled, the flesh twitching as if veined by convulsions, makes even the hardened shudder, and it is man in this mood who wages extermination in their ranks.

The hyæna, evil-looking and not of nature's best, is not so destructive, but thievishly inclined; it can boast the best bone crackers of any animal. I have seen the marks of its teeth on the spring of a steel trap in which one was caught.

Even Nature, in all her wondrous creations, has been unkind to one of the most beautiful and coveted of animals. Take for example that noble beast the greater kudu, amongst sportsmen eagerly hunted. And yet there have been many instances of the horns of two bulls in combat interlocking in their spiral curves and both animals dying, helplessly locked by their own devices.

N

Crocodile

IT is strange there should be a common enemy to both man and beast, but it is so, in that hideous monster the crocodile. It can be ably described as a loathsome beast, unloved and feared by all, and is found in most of the inland rivers and lakes. He is gifted with enormous strength and able to pull a full-grown cow into the water with ease, grabbing it by the nose with his terrific jaws, which are fitted with a cruel and useful set of teeth which interlock, and, to put it mildly, " What they grip, they hold." I have seen and heard their jaws grip together like the crack of a vermin trap, and woe betide the one who ever gets gripped !

That they are powerful and fast swimmers can be judged by the fact of their ability to catch fish, and what hope could even the fastest swimmer have to keep out of their reach ?

In their span of life the crocodile is supposed to surpass all others, and they grow to hideous dimensions. Some of the real old fellows seen in the bays from Lake Victoria are of unbelievable girth and present an altogether revolting appearance. His forefeet are armed with sharp nails which he uses for fixing the animal caught, while he rends it asunder in his evil jaws.

When I was camping near Butiaba, on Lake

Albert, I was interested and surprised to hear the harsh grunts emitted, as I had not heard him do so in the inland rivers. Their jaws are capable of expansion similar to the python, and are capable of devouring the body of a human being in its entirety. Their principal food is fish, but in many of the streams the larger and lazier animals prefer to lie near game trails and catch the unsuspecting as they come to drink. That animals know their great danger I have witnessed in watching a water buck coming to drink. He stood looking intently at the water before venturing forward; cautiously he approached, but standing as far from the water as possible, when he stretched out his head to drink. While watching I saw and heard the splash as the crocodile with a sudden movement endeavoured to sweep the animal into the water with a vast sweep of his tail. The water buck was quicker and bolted back from the river and fled into the adjoining bush. This happened at 5.30 in the evening. I am of the opinion that they are not so successful with this stroke, which is not so well timed, but this may be on account of the water being shallow. Animals, when drinking, always prefer it to deeper water, where usually the banks are steeper. That I have seen a second similar attempt, in which my gun bearer was the attacked, formed my theory, to which I will refer shortly.

Some of these African monsters reach up to twenty feet long, the average big one being about fourteen feet, weighing over a ton, girth about seven feet. I tried with the aid of twenty boys to pull one of these dead monsters on to the sandy bank at Kibanga on Lake Victoria and failed miserably on account of the dead weight. This may seem an exaggeration, but there was no one more surprised than myself at the failure in the attempt to pull it out.

The female, equally good looking, lays over fifty eggs, which are usually deposited or buried in a sand bank adjoining the lake or stream. These are hatched by the temperature of the sand, and when the young free themselves from the soft sand they take to the water immediately.

During severe drought I have seen crocodiles huddled together under embankments, usually near the washed roots of a tree, in the advanced stages of hibernation, their saggy, scaly skins adding to their hideousness. When I found them in this condition there had been no water in the stream for four months, and though I shot the outfit they were still capable of movement and could have lasted easily a similar time. They are quite capable of staying under water up to fifteen minutes, and it is fraught with grave risk and danger to attempt to bathe within half an hour of sunset. Even though they may feed at any time, this is usually the time they prefer to do their general catching and also the time when bathing is indulged in. To the unaccustomed eye the outline of a crocodile, swimming or stationary, might be taken for a stick. You see the lumps denoting his cunning and unglad eye and the rigid line, his back.

Here is where the telescope sight scores and gives
you a target that the naked human eye cannot.
When shot in the water, they sink and must be
lost unless you take trouble and probe the bottom,
if this is possible, which as a general rule it is not.
He will not float to the surface until a lapse of three
or four days, at the end of which time he floats
belly up, a decomposed mass, with a stench un-
bearable. I know of none worse, and your next
and best move is to torpedo him on the water line
with a bullet and re-sink him.

In several parts of Africa natives eat and relish
the eggs of this voracious reptile (but then, I have
seen them eat snakes and all living things). The
principles concerned in this affair, I am afraid, are
" agin " the appetite of the ordinary human.

I have heard of the Loch Ness and other monsters,
but they all seem to end at that, and now I would
see what monsters the second largest fresh-water
lake in the world—Lake Victoria—contains. This
is a most beautiful lake studded with many islands
of wondrous beauty and a few rare and beautiful
animals. The tsetse fly, the carrier of that dread
and fell disease " sleeping sickness," was up to a few
years ago rampant on these isles. Natives, the
inhabitants born and bred there, would not leave
their haunts any more than the game thereon, until
forced to do so by the arm of the law trying to
extend their life below. This plague—it is closely
allied—caused the deaths of many thousands of the
island dwellers. Since then times have changed
and now the brains of science have found serums to

combat and even cure, if in its early stages, the most dreaded of all diseases.

With all the hate attributed to these hideous creatures there is no doubt as to their general cowardice when surprised away from home; by this I mean even 100 feet from the water. On several occasions I have been hunting, scouting round the heavy bush of several of these lone and uninhabited islands, and practically walked on the top of them. Others I disturbed have gone slithering past me, their horrible eyes watching intently as they moved within a few feet of me. At the first shot old, fat, half-blind, enormously girthed brutes have not taken the slightest notice of me, and if in their wake they will try to dodge and show no sign of attack. Again, the reverse when I have approached and wounded them from a canoe, and on getting to them they have attacked viciously, using their tail with determined results. This is certainly dangerous sport, as it is most difficult to shoot with any accuracy from a wobbly canoe, and accidents always seem to happen so easily.

Returning to my Lake Victoria monster hunt. I camped at the edge of their vast inland sea, comprising twenty-eight thousand square miles, at Kibanga, a small, unimportant clearing. Scouting on the other side of the lake, I saw some very large crocodiles, but the time crossing the bay and returning did not allow me sufficient time to look them over as I wished. Returning, I arranged to shoot a hippo next morning and take it over with me as bait, using an outboard motor attached to a canoe to do the towing. Everything worked satisfactorily. I had no difficulty in shooting the hippo ; waiting an hour for it to float, I amused myself shooting duck. It was here that I saw and secured specimens of the pigmy goose.

Finding my hippo, I attached this on to a rope and towed along perfectly, practically making no difference to the Johnson's pulling powers. The distance across the bay was about fifteen miles, and I was hopeful of attracting the great reptiles from many miles around. With the aid of a number of natives the hippo was pulled clear of the water and near a large tree, where I was prepared to sit and watch, if necessary, for the next two days. With the natives cutting branches to arrange my platform, not a crocodile was seen, evidently disturbed by the noise of their axes.

After completion, and the natives had cleared off, I made myself comfortable, and here I had a great opportunity of studying Nature at her best. Kingfishers of several varieties and other aquatic birds kept skimming past, swerving off at the sight of the dead hippo. My platform was twelve feet above the hippo, and I had my hide hidden as carefully as possible by pieces of branches taken from the same tree. Within an hour I could see the crocodiles coming from all directions, the backs of the older ones sticking up well above the water, and swimming on the surface at great speeds. The majority of these animals came up to within thirty yards or so of the bait and stopped, eyes intent on the meat. This continued throughout the afternoon and all

that night. Knowing that the hippo would de-
compose in keeping with these reptiles' taste, I
resolved to wait there another day, and was well
repaid.

I was chewing at some kind of biscuits about
8 a.m. when I saw a colossal crocodile coming
straight out of the water towards the hippo. He
did not seem to trouble about the hippo, but I was
amazed when I saw such an animal come out, as
I had never previously seen any crocodile with
such an enormous girth. He walked out well up
to his feet and commenced sniffing all round the
hippo, even crawling up the side of it. I was sorely
tempted to shoot, but wanted to study him in detail
before doing so. I watched him pull and actually
saw the hippo move, which had taken twenty boys
with difficulty to get ashore. This act sealed his
fate, and I fired, hitting him where the head joins
his neck, and he died on the spot. From now on
I shot at least twenty of these beasts as they came
on, offering the easiest shots imaginable, many of
them sinking like stones in the water within a few
yards of the shore, air bubbles and blood rising from
their dead bodies. That is the easiest way to secure
these reptiles there is no doubt, and I am convinced
that up to one hundred a day could be accounted
for in Kibanga bay.

That afternoon natives came along on hearing
the shooting and assisted me in skinning the huge
first beast I shot, which was easily the largest of the
vast number seen. When his stomach was opened
it was found to contain a large number of pebbles,

which are evidently used in digesting his food. In many others have been found the gruesome relics of native ornaments, the tell-tales of many lost who never return. The fact remains that in some places the natives are able to call certain crocodiles by calls or the clapping of hands, and it is possible that some of the native burials are conducted in this way, similar to my theory of training certain man-eating lions. It is certainly fraught with danger to sit close to the water near the low banks of any stream infested with crocodiles.

I had been shooting elephants in the Kisii district, and on completion camped by a bridge on the Gori stream, which is generally shallow apart from some deep pools. My safari arrived at this place about 4 in the afternoon, and after pitching camp, my gun bearer and self commenced fishing in a pool within fifty yards of the bridge. There was a flat stone overlooking the pool about two feet above the water, and my gun bearer sat on this and commenced fishing. Now I had never seen any crocodile in this stream previously, but as it flows into the great Lake Victoria it is quite in the bounds of possibility that these brutes find their way up when the river is in flood and remain behind in the deeper pools.

We had been fishing for ten minutes or so without any luck when I suddenly saw a terrific splash in the water under my gun bearer and at the same moment the green ridge tail of a crocodile smacked on the rock where he sat, and the vile cruel head with jaws partly open was below him. It appeared to be in the form of a crescent, and its mode was evidently to swipe him off the stone with its tail into the pool and seize him with its enormous jaws. The gun bearer, an old soldier, used to the bush and its beasts with their cunning, evidently saved himself by throwing himself backwards as the tail of this beast hurtled its lash at him. I was only a distance of ten yards from him when this happened and immediately rushed to the scene of attack. The boy was too surprised at this daring attempt to grab him and looked at the wet mark on the rock where the tail had struck a few seconds earlier. Grabbing my rifle, we looked in the direction he had disappeared, but not a sign of the beast. Presently, however, my bearer pointed to the other side of the pool, and there under the shade of a green branch practically resting on the water were the unmistakable lumps denoting the eyes of this voracious monster watching us intently. It was a difficult shot even at close range, as an inch target in water is easier missed than hit, and shooting in water is always deceptive; the bullet striking the water and causing a splash beside the object fired at often appears a hit, when in reality an inch missed is as bad as a mile.

Retreating into some bush near by and overlooking the pool, we decided to wait until a better target presented itself. We did not have long to wait. That this croc was hungry there was no doubt, and shortly afterwards we saw the knobs of the eyes appear in the centre of the pool, as well as the outline of his back. Having an excellent rest on the bush behind, I took a fine sight on his bump and fired. At the report he bent up his great head in a horizontal movement above the water, and I promptly gave him another in the junction of the neck and head, the blood rushing out in a regular spout from the bullet wound. We recovered this crocodile, which had an exceptionally fine skin, and it measured ten feet long and was small in size and girth compared to the colossal monsters in Lake Victoria. Even at this length and small girth they are capable of tackling any man or beast, and when in the water they seem to be gifted with super cunning, strength and power. The streams in Africa are always an attraction, and especially if you have been hunting under the hot sun, you find yourself near the banks, forgetting about the green-eyed monster. Compare his evil eyes to those of extreme beauty possessed by the giraffe, unsurpassed in the animal kingdom, a depth which would soften the most hardened twentieth-century hunter. Crocodile lie waiting the least suspecting, be it man or beast, and the hideous thought of ever finding yourself gripped in those jaws, fitted with rat-trap-like teeth, must fill with creepy horror even the least imaginative.

Snakes

SNAKES, revolting and crawly creatures, seen at their best and worst in the veldt, more interesting when you can examine them closely in snake ponds without the attendant risk of being bitten, call for a few remarks which I trust my readers will not criticise too harshly.

I will give my observations on these reptiles as I have actually seen them in my wide and varied wanderings into many little-known areas seldom, if ever, trod by white men. If I appear to touch lightly on this subject it is because I detest them, and have not studied them sufficiently to consider myself an authority.

Snake stories, always thrilly and creepy to the imaginative, I will not inflict on you, or those of our deep-sea serpents, but keep myself confined to bare facts.

I have shot numbers of snakes and always take a keen delight in doing so. The average African native is terribly afraid of them. A dead snake suspended by the tail and carried in their direction will make them bolt in all directions; they cannot bear them and it is with reluctance they will stoop to skin one. It may interest many readers to know that amongst our African natives is a sect of snake men in the Wanyamwesi tribe near Tabora in

Tanganyika who are not afraid of snakes and will even handle or catch the swift, deadly black mamba, one of the most poisonous snakes in the world, and get bitten without fatal results. What their anti-dote against this reptile's deadly venom is would be interesting to know, and would benefit science and mankind.

George, a hunter friend of mine I regret now past the great Divide, lived amongst this interest-ing people for some time, studying their habits, and his talks on the subject were interesting indeed. Many may imagine that this dark continent is full of snakes, and no doubt there are many, but the extraordinary thing is that you seldom see them or hear of anyone being bitten. There are, as in other countries, both the venomous and non-venomous species. I disagree with some writers on the subject that the mamba is not found in Kenya, having seen both the black and green varieties when in the southern Masai Reserve, where, incidentally, I have shot at least fifty of the spitting cobra which had been sunning themselves on the crowns of ant-hills. They are only too well known to me, and in no instance have I seen one exceed nine feet in length.

The black mamba I shot in this sector measured eleven feet long, and I will describe the incident. Motoring down a bush trail which was made by the Hon. Denys Finch Hatton and myself, I saw what appeared to me the largest snake I had seen (I do not include pythons) moving quickly into an ant-hill which was partly covered by grass and creepers.

I was interested, and as some of my readers probably do not know the method of extracting them, I will explain. Taking a two-gallon tin of petrol, I approached very quietly and poured at least a quarter of the contents down one of the main apertures and brought a thin trail of the petrol back ten yards from the ant-hill. Igniting it, the flames instantly took the trail and entered the ant-hill, causing a distinct roaring inside the burrow, the flames traversing every subterranean passage with lightning rapidity. Almost immediately that mamba came out writhing and twisting, and was shot.

This is a safe method of destroying these pests, but I will give a warning note on this subject lest my remarks are experimented with. It may happen the snake never happens to reach the open and succumbs inside, then on no account must more petrol be poured down the burrow while the hot fumes are present, or an explosion will be the result, with injuries to yourself.

When hunting elephants in the desert thorn bush between the Sabaki and Tana rivers, I have on three occasions seen the green mamba, which usually are from seven to nine feet in length. With a ·22 rifle I shot with difficulty two of these reptiles which were gliding along the branches with incredible speed. When assisting with collecting reptiles in the Congo Belge for a British museum amongst others, specimens of the black mamba were also secured, being brought to me by natives, others being caught in spring traps.

I have only seen the Egyptian cobra on one occasion near the foot-hills of Kilimanjaro in Kenya Colony, and whilst looking for a stick to despatch it, the native following me yelled out " Nyoka " (Swahili word for snake). I had already seen it minutes before and frightened it; it now slid down a hole. The venom ejected by this reptile is most deadly, paralysing the nerves, and the unfortunate victim would get little time to make his peace.

Owing to the controversy on reptiles, I made a special study of inspecting them in the museums in Durban, Maritzburg, and Pretoria in South Africa, and satisfied myself as to the species I had seen in Kenya. Usually after the rains snakes appear to be more numerous, or at least you see more of them. I have frequently come across the spitting cobra and found him much on the alert. Very often you are not prepared with a 12-bore to shoot him, and while you wait for one he slides away. I always find it better when you spot him to walk past as if you had not seen him, and at some distance get your gun and return, shooting him on the march as you walk past. This method does not give him time to escape.

I must confess that one day I had a scare from one of the vile creatures. Denys and myself were motoring down a bush track in the Mara valley, driving at fifteen miles an hour, admiring a fine bunch of water buck, when I suddenly realised the swaying menacing head of a cobra on my left side, level with my head as I sat in the car. The horrible sight of this poisonous hooded spread reptile, its cold eyes, which glistened like black beads, fixed on me, held and fascinated me in all its vileness. The time can only have been a split fraction, but it seemed longer, and when the snake's head disappeared my flesh shrunk from the normal to the goosey, when I realised I had escaped being bitten. Evidently the car tyre had touched its tail or some other place, and it rose instantly and kept pace with the car for at least six feet. We stopped the car, jumped out, and going back there was the creepy poisonous creature slithering over some dry grass. The spiteful head, which a few seconds before was so close to me, was blown from its wriggling body.

One day a party of us were sitting under some of those wonderful shady wild fig trees by the banks of the upper reaches of the Tsavo, and my old gun bearer Kombo was standing leaning against an adjoining tree, when I saw him rush forward in a state of alarm. Jumping up quickly, I soon found the cause. A cobra in the hollow of the tree hissed behind his back, and on his bolting, ejected a stream of yellowish fluid at him which sprayed his coat near the shoulders. I was interested, and watched the fluid turn darker when exposed to the air. I could only see a small portion of the snake, the point of the tail and head being partly visible, while the remainder was doubled up in the hollow. Taking my 12-bore, I fired at the aperture, and on inspecting, blood was dripping from the neck of the cobra. Trying to pull him out of the tree was quite impossible, and necessitated the use of an axe to cut away the front portion. When this was done the cobra was taken out and measured eight feet long.

That this species of snake will devour its own kind I proved one day, as I killed one of these reptiles which appeared to be sluggish, and as a rule they are the reverse, but within a few seconds it commenced to disgorge another one of the same species. I could not understand this—two snakes in one !—but it is absolutely true. The snake it had swallowed was six feet long and the swallower only a foot ahead !

When in Northern Rhodesia, near Mumbwa, I surprised a green mamba which was exactly similar to those met with in Kenya, and it reared its evil head at me from the ground and disappeared. I was unarmed and appreciated my new lease of life. That their bite is death to ordinary man there is no doubt, and it is fortunate that one's sufferings would not be prolonged before being overtaken by death.

Another poisonous and unfinished-looking snake is the deadly looking puff-adder. By unfinished I mean this reptile is bulky, sluggish, and his tail does not have the streamline finish with which nature has endowed the others. This is one of the commonest snakes in Eastern Africa, and the danger of getting bitten actually lies in your walking on top of him. I have been told that he strikes in a backward movement, but having made them strike repeatedly by the use of a stick, I can confidently say this is not the case, as they strike from any angle, the large sickle-shaped fangs giving one the creeps, as I have seen them puncture the stick I made them strike.

Frequently, when preparing a new camp, the natives, when clearing away the grass and leaves, have come across these repulsive creatures, which have made no attempt to clear on account of the noise. The largest I have seen, measuring four feet six inches, was shot in the Maungu area in the coastal province of Kenya, where they are to be found in considerable numbers.

A very beautiful snake of similar length is the horned puff-adder, which I found is met with in the eastern side of the Ituri forest in the Congo Belge, the colouring and design being particularly fine, and in this category may be ably described as deadly beauty.

I will say a few words about our largest and non-poisonous snake, the python. These huge, bulky reptiles secure their prey, usually small antelopes, by a lightning circle of their great length encoiled round them. Near the end of the tail are fitted sharp, hooklike claws, and when the tail is entwined round a tree it gives these reptiles enormous agility of spring and power, so much so that one's life could easily be crushed within their deadly embrace. Frequently I have found these creatures in a sort of stupor, the great bulge in their centre denoting an antelope inside their frame, even the horns protruding through the skin to an extent of two inches. On one occasion I dug one out of a hole near the bank of a stream, and when getting close she charged out, and the method of attack was to butt with the point of her head, which can be used to advantage. This python measured sixteen feet long, but they have been known to exceed this length.

I spoiled the length of a python one day. It happened in this manner. There were three of us present and one of our trio could always give us inches, in fact, more inches on any trophy we secured or knew. Telling my friend, also a Scotsman, that I had seen a python today at least twenty-five feet long (a romance), he listened seriously and then replied, " Only twenty-five feet ! When I was in Australia I saw one of these beasts, and can you guess what he measured ?" I could not; I was beaten and simply burst into fits of laughter. If only I could have kept serious and learned those dimensions !

But I promised my readers to keep away from snaky yarns, and I am afraid I have skipped over much of these crawly reptiles' habits as to how many young snakes they bring forth, poison glands and otherwise, and the gist of my volume will show my target, but the fact remains that although several of these reptiles eat their own species either from gluttony or affection, does not make me kinder to them, and I trust my callousness does not stamp me as cruel.

In the same category are scorpions, centipedes, tarantulas and ticks; the latter on some of our vast veldts, like the Athi and Kapiti plains, are more than a scourge.

Many years ago I hunted in these places and the

discomfort was not worth it. When the grass is high you get literally covered with small ticks, ginger coloured and otherwise, and for a long time afterwards you spend your nights in bed scratching incessantly. I used to do a considerable amount of partridge shooting in these areas with the use of pointer dogs. After the first day the dogs' coats were reversed by these insects. I tried all sorts of oils to rub in their skins, but all entirely futile, and I came to the conclusion it was cruelty to indulge in this form of sport, either to man or beast, and gave it up. I am pleased to say that these pests do not exist in our best game centres, which are further afield.

Scorpions, though bad, I do not mind so much. I have recollections of indulging in a bad habit, smoking in bed, and reaching out my hand from my camp bed to find my pipe in darkness and getting stung on the point of the finger. I don't know really what my feelings were, certainly not bright, until I lighted a lamp and examined the place. Thinking it was a snake bite, one can imagine the deep relief when I saw only one puncture instead of the deadly two of the snake. It certainly caused me much pain, but after a lapse of a day entirely disappeared. The miscreant which I killed was of the amber-coloured variety.

Camping near Kenani station on the Uganda Railway, the home of many scorpions, a friend and myself arranged our mattresses and blankets under some shady rock, as we had arrived late at night and too tired to make ourselves more comfortable.

Next morning, while waiting for our boy to bring some coffee, I glanced at my friend and I saw one of the largest warty black scorpions I have ever seen before or since, crawling up the back of my friend's pyjama coat towards the direction of his neck. I said to him—" Don't move." He sat there, not knowing what danger was beside him. Picking up a dead stick, I returned, and to my horror it had crawled on to the lapel of his coat. I did not hesitate, and with a swipe, tearing his coat, the scorpion was knocked some yards away, when it was despatched. This will show the danger and attendant risks when sleeping on the ground without mosquito nets, which in this instance would have prevented the occurrence.

I have often amused myself by pulling out tarantulas from their depths by the use of a straight twig, finding these circular holes usually bordered with web. Inserting the stick usually to a depth of ten inches and flicking it on the side of the hole, and letting it rest quietly on him, you will feel and observe the stick move by teasing him a little, and on withdrawing it, especially if a female, she will follow up and charge at the stick in a jumping manner, when she can be killed. In this manner I have killed as many as twenty of these ugly insects in an hour's spider hunting.

Centipedes in their different lengths and hues are also unattractive and to be avoided. When in camp I have killed many, but in all those years have never seen one either on my bed or clothing, their legs preferring the inside of a canvas tent which would most probably foul on blankets or clothing.

Apart from man, these reptiles have many enemies in the form of carrion birds, which Nature has provided as weights to balance her vast scales.

It used to surprise me greatly as to the short lapse of time taken by birds of the air to spot any dead animal on Africa's floor. The whole sky may appear clear and not a bird to be seen in that limitless and heavenly space. Yet far away, invisible to the human eye, are specks of life—vultures ever on the alert, floating on the arcs above, ready to come hurtling down from uncanny distances, shooting through the air with wings closed, making a noise similar to a propelled rocket, curtailing this speed within thirty yards from the ground, making an easy landing on the carcase. I have watched these voracious birds from a few yards, buffeting, fighting, and jostling to gain an entrance, which only the stronger can attain.

The marabout stork, also a carrion eater, gifted with more clearance and bill, has to content himself walking round the scene, unable to compete, and trusts to get a look in when some over-gorged vulture has backed out. That his enormous bill does not give him precedence is not in keeping with his looks. I remember sitting in the shade of a bush in game country and accidentally falling asleep, and when I awoke two hours later I saw some of these vultures watching on an adjoining tree. It would be interesting to know their thoughts, if they have any, when they saw me get up and commence walking. That they have some cunning knowledge I proved on one occasion, when I was poisoning hyænas. Poisoned meat was put down, and vultures came to feed on it. One of their number was the first to take some strychnine and died within a few minutes. Almost immediately the remainder left the carcase in one body and refused to come down again to partake of the same meal, contenting themselves with resting on an adjoining tree.

What stands out as exceptional to me regarding these birds happened ten years ago, when I did not know so much of the habits of lions as I do now. In those good old days I did not know that lions would not as a rule feed on a moonlight night. I had sat beside a zebra, and its condition was high in the extreme. A boy had stayed near this kill in the daytime to keep the vultures from eating it. On the third night's vigil I was surprised to see a lot of vultures come skimming over to my blind and commence feeding on the carcase at 1 a.m. There is no doubt this was due to their hunger and the clearness of the night, but in all my travels has proved the exception. I have heard the theory put forward that vultures and other carrion eaters may be attracted to their bait by sense of smell, but I am confident this is an erroneous impression, as the fact that these huge birds—yet specks in the sky—planing at their enormous height in the heavens, gives them a tremendous field to scan, whereas had it been the reverse they would have adapted themselves to ground level.

The snake's formidable enemy amongst the feathered world is that stately slaty-coloured species, the secretary bird, which takes its name from that peculiar outcrop of feathers which extend from each side of the head, similar to a collection of pens, behind his ears. It will attack snakes, including the deadly cobra, with impunity, and I have often seen these birds flying within 200 feet from the earth with a large snake suspended at full length from their strong claws. They are indeed powerful birds and can use their wings with deadly effect, buffeting the snake and then seizing it and smashing it in the hard earth. This bird with all his qualities and good in this world is often accused of depredations amongst the eggs and young of game birds. In the vast plains of Africa, where the secretary bird is most numerous, the game bird does not breed or exist there in the same numbers as elsewhere, and it is my firm opinion that this bird should be protected in the whole of Africa, instead of only in parts as at present. His good deeds far outweigh his misdeeds, and he should be given complete protection for his assistance and aid in wielding the broom on Africa's veldt.

CHAPTER TWENTY-ONE

The Fauna's Friends & Foes

HAVING disclosed to my readers about dangerous animals and poisonous snakes, I venture a few remarks on the present form of hunting, with which some may agree and many disagree. I trust you will not judge today's method too harshly, which I can safely say has not proved detrimental to the preservation of game, and from the humane point of view has saved them much suffering. Hurrying, " making on time," has been responsible for the evolution.

Looking a century back, you find the hunters—great men of the veldt—who went into the bush, recognising different spoor. There was so much to learn in the animals' habits and ways. To many it appeared easy; to listen to yarns and read on the subject simplified the art even further. The wind was studied, the hunter walking with slow gait, not missing spoor, sound or movement of a beast. In many instances we walked all day only to brave disappointment, and in the morn ready again for the fray—skill pitted against cunning.

In that era I admit much more killing was done than at the present time; even the females—sacred to the fauna of Africa—were not spared. In the present generation there is not the slightest doubt that the sporting spirit has not diminished. God forbid that it should be otherwise, and it must bring solace to the mind of mankind to know that the relations between man and beast should be on such a wonderful footing and foundation as today. The shooter who gloated on excessive bags, taking the full quota allowed on his schedule, is in the minority and not encouraged, but suffered. The true sportsman selecting his trophy with judgment and care, killing his animal with humaneness, sparing the female and immature, must ever remain an asset to this great sporting world and friend of the game.

The wheel of mechanical transport has revolutionised man's ideas and methods in securing game, compared to the glorious hunting of the past, and even though the former is strongly condemned by many, I will endeavour to place the point of view of this so-called " vicious " practice. The general idea today is to get the animal required in the easiest manner, with as little fatigue as possible, and here the automobile has succeeded. With the exception of the elephant and rhino, few of the other varieties of game are safe from the encroachment of this wheeled chair. This method has assisted the aged in being able to approach game centres which otherwise would be wellnigh impossible. Even the wary buffalo, in some open bush country, will rise from his slumber when he hears the noise of the car, and will invariably stick his head from cover and view it from fifty yards with undue alarm.

Before the advent of the motor car, many animals were shot at and wounded, especially the antelopes on the vast plains, which were lost, pitiful creatures, to linger for perhaps days suffering from their wounds, and eventually finding merciless release by vermin and carrion feeders. I have seen a wounded gazelle tearing across the plain, its hind leg broken and swinging, and taking all other animals in its train, several thousands running in headlong flight, a sight not easily forgotten.

The game schedule specifies a certain number of animals allowed, but it does not and cannot specify for an indefinite number shot at, wounded or lost. This is not attributed to cruelty on the part of the hunter, but due to incorrect aim. The heat waves on these open spaces no doubt do account for a certain amount of missing, especially shooting animals at long and ill advised ranges. Now, with present-day methods, the majority of animals, from the king of beasts down the line, actually view the car as one of themselves, a new addition which can do no harm. When camouflaged with grass and foliage and the nickelled parts dulled with the aid of grease and earth, game can be approached to alarming distances which can be measured in feet. Here the man or woman can shoot the animal without wounding or stampeding the remainder. In this manner ammunition manufacturers suffer, and yet with all this ease in collecting trophies, it has become so easy that at least the actual shooting has dropped by 6o per cent., and the percentage gained has been given to that wonderfully interesting arm photography. The motor car has been instrumental in allowing game pictures to be taken which hitherto were impossible a few years ago. Wounded game, though not in many instances, have previously been subjects for photography, several using this method as their only means. This form of hunting is not tolerated by our present generation.

Taking the comparisons into consideration, the outcome of a quarter of a century, I trust my readers will study the complexes from both angles, and I am only too proud to say that the motor car is amongst the majority of sportsmen not the enemy but the friend of our game, and should there still remain a few who would abuse it, these, Africa will not welcome. It must be most comforting to all to realise that for generations to come, the fauna, fostered by our present game wardens, will thrive and flourish.

Now for the foes. Having hunted and travelled over practically all Eastern and Central Africa, I have in the course of many years come in contact with all classes and conditions of natives in their own surroundings, savage and otherwise. In the former state they have been mostly interesting peoples, unspoilt by the inroads of civilisation and easily satisfied in their meagre needs. I have traded and bartered with them in the Congo and generally found the native, administered under their laws, a satisfied being.

Meeting civilisation, it is extraordinary how in many instances the natives change their entire ways and beliefs. In the backwoods they will eat any kind of meat, bled or otherwise. It is all food, except in parts—I will mention the Ruanda district, which is as I write governed under a Belgian Mandate. A few years ago, when famine overran this fertile province, natives died from sheer starvation rather than feed on fish, of which there was a plentiful supply in the rivers. Under the same category as fish they treat fowls, eggs or game, their food being milk and grains.

I have seen different tribes quarrel over decayed elephant meat, pulling up grass, chewing it and working themselves into a frenzy—as bad as any animal—doing their best to stamp, bite and knock each other out of existence, and half an hour later help each other to get patched up. It is seldom they will give each other away, and generally a waste of time to probe into the depths of their misdemeanours.

On an expedition into this territory, native implements and handicraft were amongst curios of interest collected. What most interested the native were rat-traps of the wooden spring snap type. They would even offer small tusks of ivory for one of these gins. Seeing a native woman wearing a heavy chased bronze bangle, one of the village chiefs was asked if a similar could be purchased. These bangles are usually put on girls' arms when small children, making a groove in the arm as they grow up, and they can only be removed with brutality. We had no success, but in the morning after leaving camp I heard a terrible yelling going on in the direction of the village. We covered a fifteen miles march during the day, and on arriving at camp there was a native waiting with the woman's bangle in his hand which we had seen her wearing earlier on, and now offered us in exchange for a rat-trap. Needless to say, we did not accept, saying to my friend, " I wonder what means were taken to extract it."

From the devilish to the humorous. While at Lamu on the shores of the Indian Ocean in Kenya, where there are many interesting ruins and landmarks dating back to the earliest days of Portuguese and Chinese occupation, later held by the Arabs, I accompanied a friend who was interested in curios dating back to these troublesome times, and natives kept bringing in quaint old pieces of silver, copper, brass and china-ware. My friend's personal servant—a Somali named Mohamed—who knew Arabic, assisted in getting the best and genuine pieces.

One day a native came to our camp, producing from under his kanzu, or long coat, a bleached human skull and offering it for 3d. The Somali was horrified and viewed this curio with disgust and contempt, remarking that these shenzies (native word for savages) were all devils, and he spat on the ground with emphasis. The vendor, hearing the Somali decry his ware—picked it up and went off. In the Somali's tent that night there was an uproar, when he turned in to sleep, finding under his bedding the skull which was offered to us in the morning. He was most indignant and took it as a terrible insult. Incidentally, the salesman did not show up again.

Near the small town of Lamu, once the scene of a large traffic in slaves, it was in a sense pathetic to see that once flourishing place crumbling to pieces in ruins. The fine old carved and beautifully chiselled doors, relics of the last century, the only sound remaining structures of the whole house, the abolition of slavery having sealed the fate of a once hellish trade.

There are immense sand dunes within a mile of Lamu, similar to the dumps you see in the mining areas in South Africa, and with the fine sand filtering and slipping down, exposing the relics of a gruesome past. When the smite of the sword was law, what terrible tragedies must have been enacted must be left to the reader's own imagination.

This port being the hub of the Arab dhows, offered an easy way of encouraging the natives to continue in their illicit trade of smuggling ivory and rhino horns to waiting markets, and it is now that I will label these natives, armed with bow and poisoned arrows, as the foes of fauna.

Looking at the map of Africa, the reader will observe that Kenya has a large coastal frontage, also its northern neighbour, Italian Somaliland. Now here is an easy conundrum. The last named barren land holds very few elephant or rhino, but the riddle is, where do all these elephant tusks and rhino horns which are exported from these parts emanate from? The answer is—Kenya. During the years 1929 and 1930 there were 16,000 lb. weight of ivory exported from Italian Somaliland into Zanzibar. These are alarming but true figures, and will give the world an idea as to the illicit smuggling and slaughter which is encouraged and goes on unabated.

That the Game Department of Kenya are handicapped in their work against such odds goes without saying, and it is truly wonderful that with all the depredations they have to contend with and are unable to combat, our paternal Government will recognise the extreme seriousness and bring about a better understanding regarding the policing of the frontiers, which will minimise a vicious practice.

One of the most amazing captures of this efficient department in recent years took place in Mombasa. I find it difficult to express in words the magnitude of this crime which I will term " the White Rhino Disaster." Now, many of my readers may not be aware of this animal. I will touch on a few concrete points. To begin with, it is greyish-white, not white as the name would imply, and next to our largest pachyderm, the elephant, the largest land mammal in the world and taller and heavier than its black cousin. It does not occur in Kenya, the last strongholds of these fast disappearing animals being in Uganda, the Southern Sudan and Equatorial Africa. It would be interesting indeed to know where this illicit killing of these mammals goes on, which must have sorely depleted their ranks. In several parts of South Africa it used to be most numerous, but in the last century extermination sealed its fate, only a few survivors remaining in isolated swamps. Compared to the black rhino, this animal is generally inoffensive.

In recent years the animals have been strictly protected with a view to allowing the few remaining to build up their numbers again and so save what must surely have been a bulky white memory. It is doubtful if their numbers in Uganda exceed 300 animals. In April a large consignment of rhino horns appeared at the coast for shipment, amounting to 640 lb. weight of white rhino horns, actually the deaths of 125 of these very rare animals. When the merchant was caught, it was found he had a forged permit allegedly from the Congo, covering the export of 2,000 lb. weight of these horns. It was lucky that the Game Department, being suspicious of this huge number of horns, inspected the consignment as it was on the eve of being shipped, and would consequently have not been discovered. I have said enough on this loss to the world at large, with which those interested in the fauna of Africa will sympathise.

Taking Kenya as the hub of the native poacher's wheel, where the majority of these ill-gotten gains are exported or taken from, I will place before my readers some true facts showing the habits of this fraternity and the methods employed in killing and evading the arm of the law.

Tusks of ivory and rhino horns, the former from the days of the ancients, have always been a marketable commodity lending itself to the manufacture of personal and other requirements. During the year 1925, ivory commanded the large price of over £1 sterling per pound, a striking contrast to the year 1933, when the price dropped to the low

P

figure of 4s. 6d. per pound, and this for tusks of the best soft ivory weighing 100 lb. each, hard ivory being practically unmarketable.

Lastly, rhino horn, in great demand in the East and Far East, in 1929 reached the colossal price of more than 42s. per pound, or nearly £5,000 sterling per ton. In 1933 the price fell to 12s. and 55 cents per pound, the latter having gained and lost in popularity on account of its supposed aphrodisiac properties. Is there any wonder that on account of the profit gained these animals should not be left unmolested. Native poachers having been encouraged and fostered by the undesirable elements undermining the foundation of the best stronghold in Africa of these truly sporting beasts, the trader in this cursed contraband traffic is undoubtedly responsible and should be treated similarly to those dealing in opium and other dope. Deportation would meet the case and save the animal.

It is interesting to know that the old treaties of 1840 made between the Arabs and the Giriama natives in Kenya were completed over so many tusks of ivory. In those days as a rule they preferred only the portable tusks of 60 to 70 lb. weight on account of their ability to carry them. This is most probably the reason why so many elephants exist today in Kenya carrying heavy tusks weighing considerably more than 100 lb. weight in each tusk.

The premier poaching tribes in Kenya today are the Waboni and Wasanye; both are expert in the use of the poisoned arrow, and their fields are that vast area extending from the Sabaki to the Tana rivers. The Wasanye tribe probably do not number more than 4,000 souls and their only interest in life is following herds of game, which they secure by the use of traps and their deadly arrows. As they live a hard life, ever on the move, sleeping where and how they can, it is not to be wondered at that they are an unhealthy people, consumption being rampant amongst them, which will in time destroy them. The Government has done much to try and make them alter their ways and take up agricultural pursuits instead, but this has not met with a big degree of success. The fact that poaching convictions of natives amount to nearly 500 per annum will testify as to their methods of living.

The Game Laws in Kenya were introduced in 1901, and it is wonderful how the animals have survived during these fateful years when they have been hunted and persecuted without mercy. The expert poison manufacturers are the Giriama tribe, who live in the same localities, and it is surprising to know that their hut tax of 12s. each, which is paid to the Government administration, is secured from the sale of poison and generally known as the Miti Kodi, meaning the tree tax. The method employed in its manufacture is to take the roots and chips of the acranthia tree and boil it for three hours until the sap has been extracted, adding to it the juice of the cactus tree to make it sticky, when it will adhere to the metal shaft of the arrow. This poison acts on the nervous system and death follows due to paralysis. An elephant or rhino usually within a few minutes of being hit with one of these poisonous missiles suffers from acute diarrhœa, and death overtakes the " stricken " within four miles, the meat suffering no ill effects from the result of the poison.

There is a considerable trade done in the manufacture and sale of this black poisonous substance, which is in great demand in Eastern Africa, and I am convinced it is even traded as far west as Mwanza in Tanganyika Territory. The manufacture of this poison is strictly prohibited, but with the few arms of the law available, the difficulty is to enforce it, and so the nefarious practice breeds unabated.

The lords and masters of the Waboni tribe also encourage and force the poaching habit on their less fortunate fellow men by holding as hostages their wives and girls until the tusk or more of an elephant are forthcoming, and if a 100-lb. tusk is produced the poacher benefits to the extent of a cow or the return of his wife. That there is proof of Africa's best elephants falling victims to the arrow is evinced by some wonderful tusks which have been taken from the natives in recent years, three pairs, to my knowledge, weighing 179 and 165 lb., one pair of 169 lb. each, and a third of 148 and 150 lb., apart from many pairs weighing up to 250 lb., while the 100-lb. tusk is frequently met with. These weights I admit are exceptional, and in no part of Africa can such big elephants be found today as in the Tanaland Province in Kenya. For many years to come these fine tuskers will be found, and I sincerely hope when they must be killed they will fall to the bullet of the sportsman rather than to the propelled poison of the poacher. These thieves in the bush usually bury the tusks for some time before transporting them to the medium who will eventually get rid of them to the best advantage.

It may interest many to know that ivory buried in cool and wet sand near the Sabaki or Tana rivers will keep in good condition for the long period of ten years, whereas in other earths rot and decay will render them useless in the course of a few months. These poachers usually work in organised bands of a dozen or more in each, each gang having their arrows distinctly marked on the steel shaft, which would give proprietorship to any animal found dead. These arrow marks are known to other members and there is a code amongst themselves—honesty amongst poachers.

It would be quite useless for a few Government Game Scouts to try and apprehend such a mob as these. There is the instance of a small game scouting patrol proceeding down the Sabaki River and seeing a poacher in a tree, in the act of taking out honey. The three scouts, knowing this native to be a wanted poacher, waited at the foot of the tree until he came down. Eventually he did so, and imagine the scouts' surprise when they looked behind and saw themselves covered by the bows and arrows of several more poachers. They had no option but to let the native go, as had they interfered, they would undoubtedly have been " arrowed."

In these vast and little-known places, much yet untrodden by the white man, roams the poacher, and it is like looking in a haystack for a needle to find him. When the inland pools are dried up, he has to confine his activities to the main rivers, his movements being somewhat restricted. Practically all their shooting is done on moonlight nights, when the thirsty animal comes to quench his thirst. The natives find these places and usually hide on rocks or in trees, shooting the animal in the intestines at the short range of twenty yards. These natives are very good shots indeed with the bow, and I have seen them shoot a bird at fifty yards range without difficulty. The reader can easily imagine they never miss such an enormous target as the elephant or rhino.

Up to a few years ago the Government of Kenya used to pay the natives 4s. per pound for any tusk found and produced, and poaching was a flourishing industry.

To prove this assertion was justified by the bare facts that during three years 2,258 tusks, equivalent to 1,129 elephants, were handed in " as found " for the reward offered. Forsooth—1,129 slaughtered sheep, leaving their tusks behind them, the heaviest tusk being handed in at Garissa, weighing 152 lb.

I cannot understand the " powers that be " being so short-sighted as not to know what the result of this fallacy would be. It meant idle and drunken natives, coupled with harassed elephants. The Wakamba tribe of poachers increased out of all proportions, and their bands of supposed honey finders (which would pay their taxes out of this commodity) were for several years shooting "found" elephants, until the Game Department persuaded the Government to discontinue the vile practice.

That the game in Africa has been responsible for attracting sportsmen from all over the world can be judged by these figures. I will refer to Kenya Colony—probably second to none in Africa today. The amount derived by Government from sporting licences for seven years recently reached the satisfactory figure of over £70,000. Out of this sum, nearly 50 per cent. was contributed by the overseas visitor. The proceeds from ivory and confiscated rhino horns in the same period amounted to the colossal figure of £74,2000 sterling. From the latter figure nearly 70 per cent. was taken from the coastal province.

These figures will convey to the reader what a fine asset the game is to the country, as the money spent by the sportsmen, apart from the purchase of licences, is indeed considerable, and benefits a large community, and as these expeditions are not to the detriment of the game, but a boon to the Colony, they should be fostered and encouraged.

That these bands of poachers do not always have it their own way was proved by an instance when a determined gang of eleven native poachers arrived at a certain water hole where elephants were in the habit of drinking. The scene of this tragedy was within a distance of twenty miles from the Sabaki River. During the night a herd of elephants came down to drink, all the natives being asleep. This herd, on finding their natural enemies there, became an infuriated mob and attacked, killing nine out of the band, only two escaping. It is most probable that the water holes were drying up in the whole area at this period, which made the temper of these beasts all the more severe.

The natives will at times eat the raw flesh of the elephant, and I have even seen them drink the spare water which the dead elephant carries in his stomach, and on two occasions the native was violently sick afterwards from the results.

In some of the distant parts I have come on the elephants' drinking places fouled with dead locusts, and the elephants appeared to have left immediately, as they have an intense dislike and fear of the sharp, spiky legs of these insects.

Where elephants have found the biting driver ant, it is surprising how these tiny insects can aggravate the large six-ton mammal, making him crash through bush to dislodge them.

Native poachers who have shot elephants with the bow and arrow from trees have informed me that frequently if the elephant hears the twang of the bow being released he will often rush back, and should he be lucky in finding the native by sight or smell, will deliberately pull down the tree and grab the native, killing him instantly. That they accuse the bull at times of actually getting a piece of wood and throwing it with an upward movement with the tip of his trunk in their direction, I am rather inclined to doubt.

Some of the natives' methods of trapping are

cruel in the extreme. One of the worst I know is, where the elephants' beaten and used track is found, when he comes to drink under cover of darkness, a fallen tree has been placed diagonally across the path, which necessitates his lifting his front leg over it. On the other side is placed on the earth a flat board in which are studded six strong arrow heads with iron necks measuring about eight inches long. These are heavily poisoned, and one can imagine this animal's weight coming down on these sharp-pointed torture instruments, causing him to fall an easy and suffering victim.

Another cruel device, which is usually arranged near the edge of the river at the drinking place, is a foot snare. The sand is usually hollowed out to a depth of three feet and the snare, mostly made of one-inch thick plaited giraffe hide, is ingeniously placed on top of a wicker circular frame, and when the elephant treads on the frame the noose is automatically released on the leg of the unfortunate beast. The log attached to the other end is not buried, as in similar forms of traps, and weighs about 500 lb., but is left near the trap and usually elephant dung thrown over the length of rope, about five feet in length. When the beast trapped finds its leg noosed it makes a rush, and this against the weight of the attached log pulls it taut, when the terrified animal tears off with the attached log behind. This leaves a trace of the direction in which he has gone, and is easily followed up next day. There is always a chance of the log being caught up in the bush and the strain breaking ordinary rope, but the strength of this giraffe-hide rope is great and the chances of escape remote. The natives follow this trail and usually come up with a tired and worn-out animal, when the deadly arrow or spear will finish the horrible deed. These traps are largely used by the Waboni tribe and are made in different sizes, according to the foot of the animal required to be caught.

Bringing these poachers, who are imbued with the deepest cunning, to book has often taken a long weary time. In one instance, C. G. MacArthur, of the Game Department, knowing that ivory and rhino horns were being smuggled out of this Colony under his nose, was practically powerless to stop the practice, the trophies leaving the port hidden in bales and in the most cunningly thought out places. After a lapse of three years, the gang, including an Indian, a Somali and a Barawa, were actually found with the amazing number of 265 rhino horns in a store. The store was empty, apart from the spikes of these 132 rhinos, with a notice board on it, " To Let," and a cheap sixpenny padlock on a flimsy door. That these horns came from Kenya and Tanganyika territories there is not the slightest doubt, and this will give an idea of the numbers of animals shot, as for one consignment captured, how many get through ? Unless this was so, the nefarious trade would cease to exist.

It seems incredible to realise that in the past six years 8,000 lb. weight of ivory and 6,000 lb. weight in rhino horns have been confiscated by the Game

Department in Kenya, and it is an outstanding performance on the part of this most efficient arm of the law.

When hunting elephants in these parts one had to exercise the greatest care in using a game trail, especially one which led to or from water, on account of the number of traps, which were constructed of a rough bow and poisoned arrow, operated by a trip string, and 100 per cent. deadly.

Near a water hole named Pika Pika, where many animals were forced to drink during excessive drought, as many as 1,000 of these infernal devices were used to shoot the wary or unwary animal. Their usual methods of marking the place where the trap was set were by means of a small cross made by the tips of two wild sisal leaves, transfixing them and laying them in front of the track at a distance of thirty yards. Even these did not assist the trappers at times, and one meets quite a few lame ones amongst them.

Near this water hole were the gruesome remains, the skins of elephants, buffaloes, giraffes, kudu, and nine lions. Nothing could escape these path snares, and they were usually arranged at distances of 100 yards between each. The Game Department have now absolutely prohibited the use of these traps, and hence their big list of convictions to try and stem this indiscriminate killing and trapping.

In the early stages there was so much game killed that the natives could not consume the meat, and later on these trappers were reduced to eating vultures and jackals, their other supply having failed.

They hold the buffalo in great dread and fear, and it is not infrequent to see a native and a buffalo each going rapidly in opposite directions, believing in space between.

One of the most ingenious excuses I heard was when the educated native was captured with a sack of rhino horns, and asked how he came by them. Yes, he had found them, but had the Game Officer never heard of animals shedding their horns? He was probably one of the enlightened and had been studying the habits of the Scottish deer.

Then there was the Arab with his large trunks placed on the deck of the ship due to sail an hour later, and he did not venture far from them, actually sitting on them. When asked to open them, the cut portions of seventy-five rhino horns were disclosed. And so the hellish trade in this line continues.

Another dangerous gang in this illicit traffic was captured when a Barawa native chief and fourteen of his underlings, who had their headquarters at Mariakani, a large village on the Kenya railway within forty miles from the coastal town Mombasa, were caught. This place was the meeting of the cross-roads, which cut into the heart of the haunts of these fine beasts, and rhino horns, being a portable commodity, were collected in formidable numbers. When the gang was captured at Malindi, on the coast, they were found to be in possession of the heartrending number of 218 rhino horns, weighing 955 lb., and at that time worth the sum of £600 sterling.

Heavy fines were inflicted and the horns confiscated, the bright part of this valued find being darkened when it came to light that this was the second portion of the consignment, the first having been successfully exported. Here were the deaths of several hundreds of these valued beasts.

During the last few years, in the animal world, some interesting occurrences have come to light. Many have heard of the white elephant in India, but it may interest my readers to know that a white albino specimen was shot by Mr. Cunningham, a well-known hunter, a few years ago, in the Laikipia district in Kenya Colony. The skin and hair were white and the eyes pink, a distinct form of albinism. Also, a cow elephant was shot by the same hunter which was found to be carrying twins. There was also the unique discovery of the third tusk of a three-tusked elephant, which is probably one of the most unusual incidents known to natural history.

Worthy of mention is an interesting case which occurred when Mr. Dawson was shooting elephants under a control scheme in the Kisii area. He was in the act of approaching a herd of these animals when he was charged by an extremely angry rhino, and to save himself had no option but to shoot. As dusk was approaching he left the rhino, returning for it next morning. Imagine his surprise when he discovered that the herd of elephants had found it, dragging it to a distance of 100 yards, and then covered its carcase with branches. The weight of this full-grown rhino was considerable, at least a ton, and the effort was certainly no mean feat. This is the first and only time I have heard of a similar occurrence. It is a trait of the elephant when having killed a human being, to cover the body and bury it from his gaze, but I was more than surprised they would apply the same method to an animal which they had not killed.

Returning to champion the rhino cause, the suppression of the poaching and indiscriminate killing will take considerable time, hard work and patience, before he is immune from the attack of that tsetse fly, the native poacher. These natives move about in the bush with much the same rapidity as the animals themselves. They will feed on the berries and roots, and this will suffice until they are able to kill or trap some unlucky beast. It brings home the unending war of native versus beast, and the long odds of ninety to ten against the latter. The difficult problem is what steps or drastic action can be employed to combat this non-ending war on these sporting beasts.

Over Kenya's border is the Italian Somali, ever ready to do business and assist the poacher in finding a market for these wares. He is one of the principals in a cunning combine who can export trophies of value with impunity under the nose of the Government from which they were stolen. The Game Department is aware that the principal buyers are certain traders of the Khoja and Bohora community, as well as the Barawas and Somalis of Italian territory. It seems—I will repeat myself—a hellish business that war on African fauna must continue, and the pachyderms' commander-in-chief handicapped on account of his small handful of men to stem this " second to slave traffic " trade. Contrary to expectations, the motor car in the sportsman's hands has proved the animals' friend, and is responsible for the camera or cine replacing the rifle. The hunter who shoots for trophies has never been a detriment. He is an asset who selects his trophies with judgment, picking off the old animals which have usually run their course.

Should my remarks and figures assist in bringing pressure to bear on a noble cause, assisting that worthy body who are ever hopeful of the tide turning against the poacher, forcing him to abandon the manufacture of deadly poison, the twang of the wicked bow-string will cease, enabling the animals to roam and drink at will.

CHAPTER TWENTY-TWO

Heavy Calibres versus Medium or Light

A FRIEND of mine has asked me, before concluding this volume, to expound my unbiased views on rifles and ammunition which I have found in my experiences the most suitable for large and small game hunting in Africa.

I am aware that this chapter opens up a large field for controversy, irrespective of professional hunters, on which subject experts probably differ. It is naturally quite feasible that sportsmen have their own ideas, these being also based on their personal experiences.

In these concluding remarks I will therefore confine my pen to assisting the younger generation of sportsmen.

Guns and rifles have been my only hobby since a boy of nine years of age, and I have always taken the keenest interest in anything pertaining to their improvement, shooting qualities and otherwise.

My spare hours have invariably been incomplete without reference to the respective merits claimed of new weapons versus the old. Makers' lists have from time to time given me endless interest, and my bedside table has always found a welcome site for their booklets when I could find time to peruse their descriptions and claims.

The material on modern weapons is limited, and

much as I would like to explain more fully, this would necessitate my entering into the field of technical detail, so I will confine my pen to the fringe of a much discussed subject.

My facts are entirely the outcome of practical work in the field over a large number of years covering five different territories in Africa. During that period I have used, with very few exceptions, practically every calibre of rifle burning smokeless powder, from the ·577 down the line to the nimble ·22, and consider this sufficient authority to allow me to express my opinion.

Common sense will instruct us that although a certain small bore rifle will kill a dangerous animal, yet it is not to be considered good enough to stop a charging one, as the weapon must be adapted to the kind of hunting required of it, and no amount of discussion can ever make the smaller bore equalise the feats of its bigger brother.

The modern ·22 rifle firing the Hi-Speed brass cartridge and a 40-grain bullet will kill a lion or zebra at five yards by brain shots, but this is no criterion, and does not justify this excellent little weapon as a big game rifle. The light or medium calibre rifle, from ·275 mm. to the ·375, can never embody the qualities of a heavy Express ·475 No. 2, any more than the average woman could exert the same strength as a strong man. It is of paramount importance that rifles should be adapted for killing animals according to the makers' claim. I definitely state there is a vast difference between shooting an undisturbed and " peaceful "

Q

dangerous beast, compared to stopping an infuriated charging one, wounded or otherwise, which only its death can stop. The professional big game hunter (by this term I allude to the hunter who acts as guide and organiser of a shooting party) has to consider himself last and give all human protection possible to the client he accompanies. This means safety first, and the rifle which can be easily handled, and is capable of delivering the most smashing blow, is considered best. For the hunter who hunts alone, he will invariably use the rifle he fancies, usually a medium calibre magazine type. I have nothing to say about his choice, as he knows the damage he is capable of doing with it. Where the visitor—man or woman—comes up against dangerous game, and the hunter in his capacity fails to stop a charge, and damage ensues, his profession comes to an abrupt end.

Rifles and ammunition have improved enormously during the past century. With the earlier weapons using black powder, the hunter after firing had frequently to wait or step aside until the column of smoke cleared, and the cloud emitted must have at times obscured the hunter from the hunted.

It may interest the reader to know that the rifled barrel came into being as far back as the fourteenth century, and in those bygone days what crude conceptions compared to the exquisite works of art, death-dealing pieces, turned out by manufacturers at the present time.

During the past fifty years there has been little improvement in the heavier calibres of double

Express rifles, and in principle this will show the acme of perfection these arms have attained.

The bulk of my hunting experiences has been on all species of dangerous animals, and the fact that in my expeditions I have seen so many determined beasts at times difficult to stop has proclaimed me a heavy bore enthusiast. The largest calibres are low velocity, which means the bullet travels at a slow rate of speed compared to the modern Hi-Velocity weapons. Nevertheless, on one occasion when I had a bad mix-up amongst a herd of truculent elephants, and I shot my way out, the rifle barrel of my ·475 No. 2 Jeffery became so hot that after firing twelve shots rapidly my left hand was severely blistered with the intense heat set up by the heavy charge of 85 grains cordite and the 480-grain bullet.

In the interests of protection and humaneness, it is suicidal and inhuman to use a non-effective weapon on tough or thick-skinned animals. Nineteenth-century methods of hunting have entirely changed with the past. I have shot elephants dead, using ·275 and ·318 calibres, but all was in my favour, the animals on open ground, wind against them, and I could choose to shoot when and where I wanted. This is distinctly foreign to following a wounded beast into thick bush, and the animal—for example, a buffalo—charges in that " determined to destroy you " fashion. You shoot straight with the small bore, but fail to stop him. The answer—he is in at your death instead. So much for the small bore rifle.

When I have seen those grave-stones marking the last rest of many hunters killed by animals, I have pondered over the calibre of rifle used defending himself against odds. The lighter rifle against the heavier animal is apt to aggravate instead of " shock," and a determined charge in cover is almost bound to result. I again lay stress on the point that these remarks apply solely in the pursuit of dangerous game, and in the sacred cause of anyone entrusted to your care.

I will mention these heavy calibres in priority as I consider best. There are several other heavies which come under this category, but my theory is— if the same price and little difference of weight in ounces applies to all, why not avail yourself of the extra or reserve striking power ?

The rifles are double-barrelled, double-trigger ejectors—·475 No. 2; ·450 No. 2; ·470.

These heavy calibre rifles weigh usually between 10 and 11 lb., admitted, but it must be understood that recoil is more or less absorbed or lessened by weight, hence the makers build these weapons to " fit the charge," as far as lies in their power, to save your shoulder from punishment.

Should the sportsman prefer a single trigger action, then without hesitation I advocate Messrs. Westley Richards for this requirement. I have used their rifles so fitted, with complete satisfaction.

It is possible there are many sportsmen who prefer a heavy magazine rifle capable of striking an equal blow to the ·470 double barrel. Then I strongly recommend the ·416 Rigby, the latter with the short barrel of twenty-five inches. I have used several of these excellent rifles in this calibre with the longer barrels, but they appeared to me unwieldy, and the difference gained in the striking power was infinitesimal. Several of my readers may be under the impression that recoil would be a disturbing factor in firing these heavy rifles. It is commonly known as "kick," and many years ago, when I knew little, but was willing to learn, I targeted a double ·577, shooting 100 grains of cordite and a 750-grain bullet, and to steady myself leaned against a tree. The "kick" punished me severely, even the skin getting peeled from my nose. That shot taught me to avoid this method of shooting a heavy rifle. I would mention that I liked the ·577 double rifle enormously. It was heavy, but when shooting against elephant it gave one a comforting push, while the report was more soothing to the ear compared to the sharp, harder bark of the bottle-nosed ·475 or ·450 No. 2.

For the sportsman who does not mind the extra 1½ lb. weight, the ·577 double is a first-class rifle. It is difficult to lay down a hard-and-fast rule on barrel length, as this must depend greatly on the height of the individual. Just as a short barrel would appear to be stumpy in the hands of a tall man, so with the short man *vice versa*. As a general average, twenty-five inches is a first-class useful length in bush work, which is usually the place this arm is mostly used, and will not be found cumbersome.

In selecting a heavy calibre rifle, it is most

essential to see that the rifle is well balanced. If not, you will never like it or shoot to do you justice. It will always have that " crowbar " feeling about it and appear to be pounds heavier than it really is. Another important point is to see that the fixed back sight suits your eye, and that you can pick it up without the " V " appearing foggy. Defective vision may mean that the back sight should be set further away from the eye to enable you to pick it up quickly, and often when you require a heavy rifle you need it badly. All double rifles should be fitted with ejecting mechanism. The makers have perfected this action as far as possible, and the time taken in ejecting is all in your favour and safety. Apart from this, the non-ejector is practically an unsaleable weapon, should you wish to dispose of it.

It is worthy of note to mention that during my stay in Africa I have never heard of a rifle accident with any of the above calibres. This speaks volumes for all the British makers engaged in the manufacture of these arms. I remember a particular case in point, when the visitor imported a ·475 No. 2 from Belgium, and on firing at his first elephant, the top rib between the two barrels sprang up with a noise like a breaking fiddle string, and curled, fouling the front sight. I was not surprised to see the expression on my friend's face change when he realised what might have happened. A small but important minor detail which so few of our makers attend to is the sight protector. Now, as everyone knows, without the front sight you can only do guesswork shooting, and sights are so easily damaged as to call for comment. Messrs. Holland and Holland, and Messrs. Westley Richards, London, safeguard this important factor by fixing folding protectors which can be covered or otherwise at will. The former's protector acts as a night sight, which is quite a novel idea. So many of our rifles, however, have only flimsy covering bands for sight protection, which either get lost or tear your fingers getting them off and on. The above-mentioned firms have certainly deserved the grateful thanks of many extended from our hunting grounds.

Loops to take sling buckles are preferable and safer than the eyes generally fixed to take the tapered straps or hooks.

Any one of the four mentioned rifles is capable of delivering a terrible message or shock to the system of the animal fired at, and if not killed outright invariably gives you a lot in hand. I have seen animals hit, and on the impact of the tremendous hitting power received, rush off blindly, and even stumble against trees, losing altogether their complete sense of direction. A dangerous beast transformed into a cowed animal. This tends to turn the balance in favour of the hunter, apart from showing a conspicuous blood trail which is easily followed.

When an animal has charged at the short range of five yards, it gives you little time to pull the two triggers of a double rifle, let alone the act of turning the bolt action of a magazine rifle, to reload which it must be confessed does take time, and valuable time is then counted by fractions. Against the lighter missile of the smaller arm the heavier bullet of 480 to 500 grains, especially if solid, holds up well even in bush, pursuing its direction through twigs with little deflection. This is a big asset in its favour, as twigs and branches have an uncanny way of getting in your line of fire. I have seen bullets spend themselves in tree stems, and yet in firing the shooter did not detect the fouling of his aim. It is in circumstances such as these, when the brain and eye work in unison and in conjunction, the rifle plays the automatic part. With the small bore rifle, there is every possibility of the bullet, pointed or round-nosed, touching a twig and getting deflected in its course, the ping of the glancing bullet betraying its misdirected flight.

While on the subject of heavy calibres, I must mention my finding of the ammunition used therein. I am proud to say that up to date I have not had the unpleasant experience of a miss-fire. That the products of Imperial Chemical Industries are beyond praise and a credit to the British Empire goes without saying. When one realises that a single miss-fire cartridge would probably mean a life, maybe mangled, these makers have every right to be justly proud of their products. I have examined different miss-fires from other rifles, but on inspection found the caps were barely dented, and the cause due to faulty strikers in the rifle. Cartridges which have been stored under questionable conditions for twenty years have been fired and the results showed a split of $\frac{1}{4}$ inch long parallel with the case near the base, and in cutting such loaded cases open the cordite was found to be in one glutinated mass, causing abnormal pressure. A deep burial would be the only suggestion to put this danger out of harm's way. I would again emphasise that the duty of these large calibre rifles is to administer a smashing knock-out blow, which will drop the animal in his tracks and save him suffering, as well as the possibility of risk to yourself.

CHAPTER TWENTY-THREE

Medium & Small Bore Rifles

IN the medium and small bore lines there have been enormous developments and improvements during the last few years. Controversy has raged on this subject, small versus big, and in all fairness I will place the latter on its merits, for the use for which it was originally designed by the makers. With these arms, their propellants have improved likewise, and the three vexed questions, today are velocity, pressure and energy.

Theoretically and fundamentally, they are perhaps more perfect than the mind of a few years ago could have conceived. I do not intend going into intensive detail, as there are many who would not be interested if I did. As long as the rifle shoots straight and kills—these are the main points. Possibly if I had to relate that the cap which on contact against the anvil ignited in less than the thousandth part of a second, or that the muzzle energy was so-and-so, and that some bullets are snub-nosed, streamlined, or boat-tailed, you would be curious and pass it at that. This is not my intention, and I will confine myself to their merits for the use intended.

The big question put up by many sportsmen is, Why carry a heavy rifle when the lighter will do the work required? Granted, with this weapon more accurate shooting can be done and the recoil is not so punishing, but a donkey cannot drag a weight compared with a horse. So be it.

The gun dealers' racks today hold selections of high velocity rifles, weapons of extreme accuracy, and joys to handle—so much for their wonderful craft. These are all excellent and all compete for the speedy destruction of the animal fired at. Between the merits of modern progressive flaked powders I will not discriminate. Whether products from America, the Continent, or Britain, they are all excellent and death-propelling. Improvements in rifle and cartridge manufacture defying further accuracy, coupled with stainless or rustless barrels, complete the destiny of destruction.

Just as British firms manufacture all the heavier calibre and proprietary calibres, etc., so do the Mauser works turn out as efficient products in Magnum form and ordinary, while the Americans still experiment on their 30·06 and the latest in loads to simplify shooting for the shooter.

With the modern weapons, the aim of the manufacturers is a good one, penetration, shock, and absence of recoil, and when shooting at even small game, such as antelopes, the presence of the latter is negligible. I wonder how many of my readers, unaware of its presence, have seen its action on the points of soft-nosed bullets getting flattened and distorted while still in the magazine of Mauser type rifles when fired. With the finest lead points this is not so noticeable, as the top of the nickel housing comes in contact with the metal, but with the medium and full tip soft points the lead assumes flattened proportions which detract from the accuracy and power of the missile in flight.

I will now touch on the medium bore rifle and trust my remarks will not be found out of place. It may be there are many who carry their own rifle and there is the remote possibility of meeting a dangerous beast, and I will name my choice in these arms and my reasons for doing so. If I have refrained from mentioning any particular calibre, I have not done so from any motive, but in my vast experience in arms I am quoting observations from weapons mostly used. I have drawn a line in calibres covering the medium bore with a limit to the 9·3 Mauser ·366. Again in priority:

1. Holland and Holland ·375 Magnum magazine.
2. Rigby ·350 Magnum magazine.
3. Mauser ·366 or 9·3 Magnum magazine.

The first-mentioned is probably too well known amongst sportsmen for further comment, and it may be summed up as a first-class weapon. I have used many of these rifles, and for lion shooting, using the 270-grain bullet with short exposed lead tip, it has great striking power, which gives telling effect. As a lady's big game rifle against dangerous beasts it is *par excellence*, as fitted with a recoil pad the kick is scarcely noticeable. Using the 300-grain solid bullet with this rifle, I have seen many elephants killed cleanly, and I can strongly recommend it. For the sportswoman's safety it is understood she is accompanied by a white hunter, who has a heavy double in reserve in case of need. The price of ·375 Magnum ammunition in Nairobi is £4 per 100 rounds, which is indeed good value.

Next in my selection is the Rigby Magnum ·350, also an excellent all-round rifle.   But in my opinion the cost of the ammunition in Nairobi as I write, being £6 per 100 rounds, is against its popularity.

Last is in this class the 9·3 Mauser, or ·366, which is one of the most largely used rifles in Africa at the present time.   This weapon has made its own popularity, and is a very fine all-round useful rifle, apart from the cartridges being retailed at the reasonable price of £3 per hundred, a big economy amongst those in its own class.   I have used this calibre in both the low and high velocity weapons on all game, including elephants, rhino and buffalo, and it is a moderately priced production which serves its purpose well.

Combining these three excellent rifles, in my opinion there is scope for improvement in the magazines of all of them.   I have seen from actual experience the tips of the soft-nosed bullets flattened and distorted in the cartridges which were housed in the magazine, while solid bullets have become loose due to the recoil on the rifle being fired. The usual procedure is, when the sportsman has fired the shot in the chamber he reloads, keeping his reserve number in the magazine intact.   After a few shots, the cartridges bang forward in the magazine at each shot, with the results already described.   On this matter being brought to the notice of the Mauser works, the German manufacturer tried to overcome this difficult matter by having a strip of rubber inserted inside the magazine face, but it did not serve the purpose after a time, due to the tropical perishing action on the rubber, coupled with the ill-effects of gun oil permeating same in cleaning the rifle. As I write, however, I am pleased to learn that this rubber insertion will be discontinued in future, as German engineers have now found a better solution in arranging flanges inside the walls of the magazine which will keep the shoulder of the cartridge in place, counteracting the rebound. In barrel lengths for all the above weapons I prefer twenty-five inches, which combines the happy medium, and a crisp single trigger pull of 4 lb.

Sighting must always be a matter of choice, but I have actually seen more accurate shooting performed using the " U " sight than the " V," as the former does not lend itself to so much error in canting the rifle, a failing of many shooters. The powder generally used in the medium and small bore rifles today is a flaked cellulose variety, which, when exposed to the open, is slow-burning, but when confined and harnessed under pressure is lightning quick; while in the heaviest calibres cordite, which has stood the test of time, is still to the fore.

Today the object of the sporting rifle manufacturers is to provide a weapon which will give more penetration and smashing power than formerly. It is doubtful if this can be improved upon, and it goes without saying that animals are killed cleanly by the results of perseverance in research. In shooting thin-skinned game—I will include all the cat family—the finest lead tip on the apex of the bullet gives the best results, and I have found it preferable to the copper expanding or split walled type.

In the lighter class of rifle, progress has produced astounding developments and high velocity marks a new departure in these deadly weapons. The big idea has been to increase the powder charge, lighten the weight of the bullet, enabling it to cover distances without altering the sight, which makes the judging of reasonable distances an antiquity of the past. One must give credit to their brains in working out mathematical problems to elucidate the evolution in these arms of the present day.

To avoid highly charged criticism between the low and high velocity enthusiasts, I will give my findings or results on the practical instead of the theoretical side, and should my opinion differ from many, I am giving it for what it is worth in the hope that even better results will accrue. With the smaller thin-skinned antelopes, the low velocity weapons actually in practice prove more satisfactory than the high, on account of the missile from the latter passing clean through the animal hit, thereby defeating its object. It is horse sense to realise that the bullet which remains in the animal in compact form, giving shock to the system and full striking force, is what the makers intended of it. But should the bullet pass through the body on account of the velocity or driving power, it means a punctured animal, and the force intended has passed on to expend its energy beyond. I have actually seen two antelopes shot in a line with this type of bullet, the first in line standing hunched where hit, and the second collapse to the impact. Here is a difficulty which can better be described as " what you lose on the swings you gain on the roundabouts."

Against a heavier body like waterbuck, lion or zebra, where tough muscle and flesh give heavy resistance, these arms are ideal and can be confidently recommended. They simplify distances, and where with the low velocity you had to raise your leaf sights according to your judgment, the high velocity overcomes this difficulty, giving a flat trajectory in several calibres up to 250 yards, which covers the general trend in ordinary shooting distances.

I have found it a good idea to have rifles shooting Hi-Velocity ammunition sighted at 150 yards, the difference in elevation shooting at 100 yards either way being infinitesimal.

An important factor in the African light is to have the front bead on the foresight made of either enamel or gold, which is decidedly preferable to the ivory tip, which gets yellow through contact with oil and is very easily broken off, compared to either of the former. Using high pressure cartridges also calls for care to see that the screw which holds the action of the rifle to the stock is kept tight, otherwise on account of recoil the top chequered wood in which the action fits will crack or splinter. This should be re-tightened up after the first few rounds fired when the barrel becomes properly embedded in the stock.

The weight of the rifle should be sufficiently heavy to absorb the recoil. The latter, as the reader may guess, is the movement of the weapon when fired moving in the opposite direction, your shoulder acting as a rebound. Otherwise it would be unpleasant to use and have a jarring effect on the system, invariably producing headache.

I have witnessed the effect of the light 150- and 180-grain missiles on the heavier dangerous animals, such as buffalo and rhino, and taken immense trouble to trace the bullets or their remnants, from the bodies concerned. With these animals, if the bullet was soft point, invariably the nickel base had parted company from the core, being found torn and curled by the impact of the heavy body, while the core had splintered into fragments, ceasing to remain a solid or mushroomed body, the existence of the small bullet, propelled with its terrific force, losing its entirety and purpose.

The solid bullets used with these rifles are also pointed to overcome air resistance, when pursuing their terrific flight, and I have found against the heavier animals are apt to deflect from either bone, or branches encountered, the ping informing you as you hear it travel in its misdirected course.

Improvements have been carried out with a view to strengthening the nickelling to stand up to the extra strain on impact, which are dubbed strong-

R

jacketed bullets. This is a move in the right direction. The knock-down blow is largely dependent on the bullet retaining its substance and course, when it will have forced its way through flesh and muscle, and carried out its mission.

Force and velocity are an excellent combination, provided the bullets do not travel with excessive speed, which carries the missile through the animal, thereby giving no apparent shock to the system of the beast, whereas, had the bullet remained in the body, its full shocking power would have been utilised.

I have listened to the impact of both high and low velocity bullets, the former hitting with a distinct click, and at the shorter ranges may not be heard on account of the lightning speed, whereas the " flup " or thud from the latter is easily audible from all ranges. Sometimes an animal may drop instantaneously, and it is advisable to be ready to shoot again, as it is quite likely he is only stunned and may get up again, and tear off without giving you the chance of a second shot. I have seen this happen on several occasions, thinking I had the beast down for keeps, and have had the bitter disappointment of seeing him clear off as though unscathed.

In mentioning a few of these light calibre rifles, I apologise for any omission, apparent or otherwise, but I will again state I have no axe to grind and my choice is from field results.

Mauser 8 by 60 Magnum-bombe equivalent ·315 Hi-Velocity.
Holland ·300 Super Hi-Velocity.

American 30-06.
Rigby ·275 High Velocity.
Westley Richards ·318 Accelerated Express.

To discuss the merits of each would take up much time, and I have no desire to go into technical details. At the least I can truly say these are all excellent weapons, and eminently suitable for ordinary shooting in Africa. The Mauser 8 by 60 must not be confused with the old pre-War 8 mm. equivalent to the 7·9 calibre ·311, as this excellent rifle has a muzzle velocity of 2,850 feet per second and a striking muzzle energy of 3,350 foot pounds, a great performance. The bullet weighs 185 grains, and to use on lions I have found this 8 by 60 calibre a deadly weapon, and pleasant to handle.

The American ·30-06 rifles are most accurate, and from the costly Griffen and Howe product to the moderately priced Remington, firing the Peters ·225 grain belted bullet, are capable of holding their own against the biggest cats.

Before closing these practical notes pertaining to arms, I would like to draw my readers' attention to a most efficient small bore rifle, a recent production, namely the Mauser ·22, with detachable magazines holding five and ten shots as preferred. This rifle is well balanced and has a full stock length. The model is M.M. 410B. It shoots the Hi-Speed Rim Fire ·22 long brass cartridge, propelling a 40-grain bullet, with fine penetration and extreme accuracy, and is incomparable with the old ·22 long, using the ·22 long copper shell. For shooting the smaller antelopes and larger game birds it fulfils a long felt want and has to be tried to realise its excellent performance.

I do not know sufficient about automatics to criticise or advise.   Having seen many of all makes and sizes, and when on two particular occasions their safety devices were being demonstrated in the bush to me, they accidentally spat fire in their sharpest barks, one of the bullets narrowly missing me, I will refrain from further comments, and touch on a favourite arm, the revolver, which I believe will continue for many years to come; and, as a guiding principle in the hand arms, I will mention two of these weapons which may be considered as being safe to handle and capable of dealing out full stopping power.   Alphabetically, they are the Colt ·44/40 New Service revolver, and the ·357 Magnum Smith and Wesson revolver.   The former is most accurate and powerful and absolutely dependable should you ever find yourself in a tight corner.   The new ·357 Magnum Revolver cartridge is the fastest yet made.   The weight of this bullet is 158 grains and is actually a ·38 calibre, and the velocity attained reaches the terrific speed of 1,512 feet per second.   These cartridges could not be used in the old ·38 special revolvers.   For wonderful accuracy and penetration they are unsurpassed.   In these arms I would suggest the barrels to be not longer than six inches.

Before quitting arms, I must fire a parting shot with any calibre of either velocity at the gun maker.

If you are feeling out of sorts in the field and not shooting as well as you might, do not throw all the blame on that wonderful artist. He may have even sweated to suit your requirements, sighting your rifle in, and many other details as you fancied. For erratic aim there are so many other causes it may be attributed to, apart from liver. Africa holds lots of heat waves, which dance and waver in front of you, and may be causing you to follow suit. There are winds, both frontal and aft, for the deadly or otherwise bullet to contend with. I am a great believer in Fate and have seen bullets raise spurts of dust all round the lucky unconcerned animal. Do not let these shots worry you. Conditions will improve and must adjust themselves in their own way from day to day, and everything in the end, without being pessimistic, will turn out in your favour. So be it.

For the sportsman or woman with impaired vision, the telescope fitted on any of the above light calibre rifles is the uncanniest and deadliest of all arms. These 'scopes are readily adjusted and the fixing lugs have been much improved upon during recent years, and the rigidity not impaired by the recoil of the rifle, which was a troublesome factor some years ago. With the rifle so fitted, for animals at distances, where with the naked eye the front sight obscured most of the object, the telescope throws out the point of aim clearly and defined, making much more accurate shooting. Against crocodiles it is a certain exterminator.

I would mention that the Zeiss 'scopes and their

fittings are excellent, and power 4 × is recommended for the African light.

While in the humour I must relate two amusing incidents which happened on the veldt. I, with my old gun bearer Kombo, accompanied a certain foreign nobleman on a shooting trip. One day we spotted a fine-maned lion sitting looking in every direction but ours—" a sitter or jam," you might term him. The three of us did a snaky stalk on our tummies, getting up within easy shot, my friend puffing badly from the strain. I was told to " Tire," but did not understand the meaning. Waiting for the noble lord to shoot, nothing happened. He then looked at me menacingly, and I understood. We shot as one, killing the lion. Immediately my sly old gun bearer rushed ahead and I could see him drawing his bushman's friend (a knife) as he did so, the knife being hidden by the palm of the hand and the forefinger, pretending to examine the lion, but in reality plunging the knife behind its shoulder to make it appear as though a second bullet wound was there.

Then there was a canny Scot who had fired at many, but failed to hit, and old gun bearer Kombo, feeling the strain, emphasising it with a clicking noise with his tongue, as a cabby to his horse, remarked in sympathy, " Bwana, you shoots m'zuri, but you shoots burre." (Translation: " m'zuri " means good; " burre," no good.)

CHAPTER TWENTY-FOUR

The African Native

THIS volume would be incomplete without some mention of the African native, who largely contributes to the success of the general expedition. Whether they may be gun bearers, skinners, motor drivers, cooks, or the happy-go-lucky porter, they are indeed masters of their craft, and without their indispensable aid safaris could not be accomplished. With few exceptions, the gun bearer will give his life if need be in the defence of his master, and what greater sacrifice could be shown from man to man, be he black or white?

The Wakamba native professional skinner, a master of his art, without whom the trophies of the chase could not be handled to satisfy the fastidious requirements of the different museums, is a testimony to the black man's skill. The perfect skinning of the animal, be it elephant or dik-dik, must be seen to be believed. There is no other tribe in Africa to compete with their efficient workmanship.

The native driver-mechanic of all tribes is to be found throughout the whole of Africa. Some are good, many indifferent, and, " as you value your life, value your car, and hope for the best."

The indispensable African cooks, the Uganda

tribe being outstanding, are capable of serving up a seven-course dinner and they seem to understand that to gain favour is " to feed the brute." They do, and thieve, both exceedingly well. They evidently think, what is good for the goose is good for the servant.

Now for the porter, the mainstay of the safari; none could do without him. On several thousand mile trips his place is perched on top of the overloaded truck, clinging with his hands and toes to the tie ropes as a monkey to a tree, and literally may be described as the pendulum of the safari clock. In the bush he excels, carrying the water and hewing the fuel, apart from being at the beck and call of all. His general ambition is to rise to the height of a mechanic, of which he usually thinks he knows all, but in reality he knows nothing. He is more than likely to fill the radiator with petrol and the petrol tank with water ! Such are the joys (?) of African safaris. On reaching a village he will drink native beer (pombe), his ideals being wine, women and song and no thought for the morrow.

An instance occurred at Mwanza, when one of these porters was missing for three days, arriving a few minutes before the departure of our safari, clad only in his shirt, and two buxom lassies of his clan accompanying him carrying, one his pants, and the other his boots, which they refused to relinquish until he had paid his fees due for board and lodgings.

When in Rhodesia I was amused at two of our

porters dancing in front of a pet baboon, and the antics of the trio were certainly entertaining and balanced.

Talking of baboons, a humorous incident came to my notice when part of the expedition comprised a sucking pig and a pet baboon. The latter spent hours daily turning over the bristles of the pig, ever looking for the unattainable and conveying the uncaught to its mouth. One day the piglet, getting fed up with the unending search, showed its displeasure by trying to escape from the hands of the baboon, who became furious, grabbed the piggy tighter by one hind leg, sniffed its bacon, and threw the squealer with disgust out of the picture.

The natives' great weakness is their love for liquor, whether of European or native origin. The latter is usually coffee-coloured, brewed from mtama, maize, bananas or sugar cane, and at the best sickly smelling concoctions.

They are withal a good-natured crowd, prone to laugh, and adapt themselves to conditions easily.

Witchcraft or the magician medicine man does not have the same sway, and with the advent of civilisation is quickly dying out, a real menace being removed, for the natives' good and betterment.

I have heard of black magic being practised in the bush by a few white men, but this could no doubt be attributed to their being under the tropical sun too long.

A friend of mine, a certain countess, informed me she actually saw this weird display; it consisted of pouring some whisky into a hole in the sand and chanting over it, while the look of the hunter's steel-grey eyes, in her own words, " scared the life out of her." I would sum up this mania as a waste of good whisky and a cause for reflection.

CHAPTER TWENTY-FIVE

Safety, Care & Cleaning of Rifles

I WILL now give my readers a few words of advice on the safety, care, and cleaning of rifles. Primarily, I will speak and lay stress on the great care which must always be exercised by anyone in carrying or using firearms of any description. To have a gun barrel aligned in your direction, either in the field, or in a gun maker's shop, empty or otherwise, tends to make you beat a speedy retreat. Accidents through carelessness have accounted for many valuable lives, and the hard and fast rule, without exception, should be that the barrel should only be pointed towards the target, or the beast or bird you wish to kill.

When following animals in heavy bush, and only one trail to follow, the hunter following the sportsman must use his own judgment as to the safe way his rifle, which is naturally loaded, must be carried, without pointing it in the direction of his leader. There are so many dangerous ways of carrying a rifle, and no gun is considered safe if focussed in your direction. Crawling under heavy foliage will test even the more experienced, because it is most essential that as you expect to meet the animal the gun must be carried loaded. The highly excitable shot is closely allied to the dangerous, and the habit of carrying the gun " off safe " is inexcusable, as the one in front requires all his vision in that direction.

With the advent of the motor-car, guns usually find a resting place at the back of the car, lying against the cushion or seat.

I say, it is an unpardonable crime to your fellow-men to transport weapons with cartridges in the chambers. Jolting and thumping are so very liable to move the safety slide forward and an accidental discharge is sooner or later almost certain to result. Cartridges can be had in a moment's notice when required, and the driver can keep his eyes on the road instead of wondering and looking to see in which way the cold steel muzzle lies pointed. Several fatal accidents have already been attributed to this careless cause, and these will continue unless the gunner insists on the vital point of empty rifle chambers.

Many car gun accidents have been caused by sheer carelessness on the part of the man concerned. In jumping clear of the car, in his haste he has grabbed the weapon by the barrel (instead of the hand grip of the stock), pulling the gun in his direction, when some obstacle has fouled the trigger, thereby causing his own death.

When natives have been left in charge of the car in which firearms were placed, their first impulse is to handle the gun, pull the triggers, irrespective of whether the gun is loaded or in which direction it is pointing.

Apart from danger in the car, there are instances where the hunter concerned has been climbing up a tree to obtain a better view of the animal. The native has assisted to push or steady him by the rifle barrels—a dreadful thought—either soft nose or solid bullets staring his posterior in the face.

An incident which might have led to serious consequences occurred when a motor-lorry was travelling on the rough stretch on the main highway between Longido and Arusha, in Tanganyika. The gun bearer and several boys were sitting on the floor of the lorry, the former having a double ·470 rifle between his knees, the butt resting on the floor. This rifle was loaded and at safe, but on the European driver negotiating a bad bump, the butt came heavily down on the floor, the jar causing the rifle to discharge its right barrel, even though the weapon was at safe. This is an exception, but with many of the rifles you find in Africa they do not visit the makers for annual overhaul, and with neglect these things will happen.

I am of the opinion that in the interest of public safety, just as the law can take action against the driver for defective brakes in his automobile, so should the same arm govern the prohibition of carrying in a car loaded barrels of a firearm, especially gun or rifle.

If you are shooting guinea fowl or other game birds, and your gun bearer who is carrying your spare rifle has to assist in retrieving them, precaution must be taken to see that he does not club the runner with your pet rifle. He will undoubtedly get the bird, but examine the stock carefully to see that the tell-tale crack does not show its presence at the hand grip, and when you slate him for the offence he will calmly tell you the bird bumped against it.

While on safety first, a few maxims to my younger followers may serve to guide them, which I will enumerate as simply as possible:

1. Make yourself a safe shot—the world can pay you no higher compliment.

2. Aim at being a close instead of a long range enthusiast.

3. Always look through the barrels before starting out.

4. Avoid using ammunition of doubtful age. Rather bury it.

5. The cause of double discharge is invariably due to the stock being too long, causing the finger to slip back, due to natural recoil, on to the second trigger.

6. It is advisable to have the left trigger pull half a pound heavier than the right.

7. Should you slip or fall, causing the muzzle of the rifle to come in contact with mud or any obstruction, unload and look through the barrels before firing.

8. If time warrants it, always reload after firing your right barrel, and keep your left in reserve.

9. Approach your danger with gun at safe and throw it off at the moment of firing. Coolness will master this lesson.

10. Learn to shoot quickly—the best shots are generally the quickest.

11. Save the animal as little struggling as possible.

12. To ascertain if dead, touching the eye will be an excellent guide. If *rigor mortis* has not set in, the eyelid will flicker.

13. Beware of the animal lying apparently dead, the movement on its side will betray the breathing.

14. Definitely unload your rifle before returning to camp.

I have seen excited shots, having their rifles on danger, bang off accidentally, due to branches brushing against the trigger on the rebound, and it is a most alarming sight to see the mark where the bullet has ploughed into the earth a few feet from you. I will confess such instances are the exception, but from time to time do happen, and I want to impress upon the younger generation the grave seriousness of such acts.

Gun accidents have invariably such fatal results, and in the field the whole enjoyment of a most promising time can be marred by such an incident. The weapon must always be carried in such a manner that in case of accidental discharge the bullet will find its resting place far from the line of man or beast.

Should there be several hunters in the bush, on no consideration should a shot be fired at any movement therein, unless you can safely see the remainder of your party. It is in places like these where one's discretion may run riot, one of the party gets separated from the others, and his movement in the foliage is taken for that of the animal hunted. It is always better to let the animal go, than take risks, and be certain you know the safe direction which your bullet will pursue. On our vast plains where there have been several parties shooting, I have heard the ping of a bullet overhead which must have travelled over a mile, and yet the party who fired were quite unaware of your presence. It is interesting to state that on one of these plains I picked up three spent bullets, but luckily on the ground.

It is a paramount rule that rifles should be kept on the safe position until you are going to fire. With the hammerless double barrel the safety slide can be pushed forward at the moment of throwing up your rifle to fire, and with the magazine the safety catch can be kept in an upright or central position when it can be turned to the left in a fraction at the point of firing. If this golden rule is observed, no accident can ever possibly take place, which is the true aim of every sportsman.

In the first hour's hunt with your visitor or companion, you will easily discover what school of sport he has taken his lesson from. With ordinary care accidents will never happen and you will not be the cause of harm to others. A few lines will not be out of place on obstructions in gun or rifle barrels, especially in the African bush.

When camping, and your rifles either stand in an improvised rack or lie under your camp bed, across the cross members, I have on several occasions found that beetles have an aptitude for building nests of mud or leaves midway up the barrel. Their fancy is more the heavy calibre rifle than the smaller, and it behoves the sportsman to make the unwritten law to look down his rifle every time he takes it out, to see that no obstruction exists. The damaging effect of such an obstacle, should the rifle be fired, would most probably prove disastrous to the shooter. These beetles are quite capable of making one of their new homes in your pet rifle barrel in two days.

Where there is a party shooting, and using different calibres of cartridges, here you have a real danger. The average native gun bearer does not know the difference between many of the smaller calibres, and they seem to have a wonderful knack of getting hold of the other man's cartridges. Two instances came to my notice where a 9·3 Mauser cartridge, equivalent ·366, was inserted and fired out of a ·350 Rigby Magnum rifle, the only damage being the extractor of the bolt being broken on trying to eject the empty cartridge, the steel grip having cut a groove into the soft rim of the ·350 cartridge case. On the shot being fired, there was a distinct blow back near the shooter's eye.

In the other instance, a High Velocity 8 by 60 = ·315 was accidentally inserted into the chamber of a 30·06 Remington rifle and fired. The recoil and shock to the shooter in this case were distinctly alarming, the bolt being damaged beyond repair, and it is surprising the shooter's cheek was not more damaged.

It is most important, where any undue force is required to turn your bolt action home on reloading, to extract the cartridge at once without

s

further pressure. Force exerted on the bolt will squash, in many calibres, the wrong cartridge home, and there is the grave danger of firing a thicker bullet up the barrel than it was bored for. I cannot over-estimate this horrible thought and risk.

With the shot-gun accidents can also happen, as was proved when I was shooting spur fowl and guinea fowl in a maize crop in the Saba-Saba district, between Thika and Fort Hall. My solicitor friend and self, with several natives, were walking the patch in line when a duiker doubled back behind us. My friend fired and the duiker went down, but the yells emitted seemed to be more human than duikerish. On our retrieving the duiker, there was one of our beaters with his pants off, yelling his loudest. He had actually been in the act of stealing and hiding maize cobs when the duiker had run past him, both getting the distribution of $1\frac{1}{8}$ ounce of No. 5 shot. His bum displayed an even pattern, and the ointment of Rs. 20 certainly worked wonders and an effective cure!

Lastly, but a most important factor, bad condition in gun and rifle barrels is usually attributed to defective cleaning, and I know of few worse sights than the inside of a valuable or otherwise weapon damaged by neglect. With heavy calibred rifles especially it is most essential that the greatest care should be taken for several days after firing them. They tend to sweat, and that beautiful dazzling polish will soon get dulled unless necessary precaution is taken.

With the present non-fouling bullets in use today in the medium and light bores, corrosion is not nearly so prevalent as a few years ago, science and skill having fathomed astounding results in anti-fouling projectiles, which has simplified cleaning operations considerably, compared to the past.

The chief damage caused to rifle barrels is due to careless cleaning and dampness. I have found for ordinary care in the field to clean your rifle after use it is most important to use the bristle brush which has been soaked with Young's cleaner or Ballistol, when the burnt residue will immediately become loosened. With three applications the barrel should have regained its perfect polish. This is the biggest enemy which rust has to contend with. Should the nickelling appear obstinate, the brass wire brush coated with similar oil must then be resorted to.

Heavy Express rifles, after firing cordite, are more difficult to clean, the nickelling being most predominant within six inches from the cartridge chamber. This is almost certain to necessitate the use of the brass wire brush, and exceptional care must be taken to see that not a speck is left. I have found Hoppes' fluid a splendid antidote for dissolving the fouling. When the barrels are thoroughly clean a thin application of vaseline inside and outside all the metal work will keep your rifle in excellent condition.

A few old tooth brushes are excellent for removing grit or other substance from the breech action, and general external use. For the woodwork, raw linseed oil used sparingly will be found specially good. It is essential that the proper size of patches are used, and here is a fault with the African gun bearer. When cleaning your rifle he will invariably try to force a larger patch than will enter the calibre without undue force. The result is—rod and patch get badly stuck. Should this happen, I will give a useful tip for removing it. Heat some Young's celebrated cleaner or 3 in 1 oil and pour down the barrel, allowing it to soak for ten minutes, and immediately repeat the operation from the other end, giving time for the two soakings to meet. In this way the stubborn rod may be withdrawn.

By far the best cleaning rod to use in camp is the pull piece unjointed celluloid steel-centred rod, with ball-bearing top, using the standard thread brush. The jointed type are a useful stand-by in case of emergency and fit easily in the case.

Amongst the best oils at the present time I find are Young's, Kleenwell, 3 in 1, and last, but not least, Neoballistol.

A good gun or rifle carefully stabled and groomed will last many years, and there is always the feel of a pet weapon, which seems to companion with you, and it will well repay you for the time and trouble expended on its upkeep.

The spirit of adventure may still flow in the veins of some who even in this twentieth century would like to be amongst the first to visit grounds not yet hunted by sportsmen. Kenya Colony still holds virgin hunting grounds, magnificent elephants, and a wonderful show of game, big and small, Nature far removed from the haunts of mankind, where the automobile is defeated by absence of roads. Here is untrammelled freedom, Nature's beverage, peaceful sleep, away from the noise and turmoil of daily bustle and strife. Surely, for the harassed, a rejuvenated life.

I have endeavoured to give the rising generation my observations and experiences, which are based on practical findings, and the outcome of over a quarter of a century, gained over a wider field than the vast majority have hunted, many of the places not previously visited by white man.

So much has already been written on confined territories, but in my opinion not enough on the wider field.

Critics may consider my views and selections dogmatic, but in the main they will, I hope, be found sound, unconditionally well meant, and unbiassed by any train of thought.

The big game hunter must always be a law unto himself, erring on the side of caution and humaneness.

Should this volume, with its thrills, provide amusement or guidance to others, my ambitions will be justified and my labour not in vain.

INDEX

279

Printed in Great Britain by
Billing and Sons Ltd., Guildford and Esher. 1938.

Additional books by J. A. Hunter

Hunter

Hunter's Tracks

Tales of the African Frontier

are available through

SAFARI PRESS INC.
P. O. Box 3095
Long Beach, CA 90803